When You Look For Me

Kevin Bonang

Pottersfield Press, Lawrencetown Beach, Nova Scotia

Library and Archives Canada Cataloguing in Publication
Bonang, Kevin
    When you look for me / Kevin Bonang.

ISBN 978-1-897426-06-7

1. Bonang, Kevin. 2. Children – Death. 3. Tanner, Tiffany.
4. Fathers and daughters. 5. Kayaking – Accidents – Germany.
I. Title.

HV6762.G3B65 2009   362.82'97092   C2008-907938-8

Cover design by Gail LeBlanc

Pottersfield Press acknowledges the financial support of the Government of Canada through the Book Publishing Industry Development Program for our publishing activities. We acknowledge the ongoing support of the Canada Council for the Arts, which last year invested $20.1 million in writing and publishing throughout Canada. We also thank the Province of Nova Scotia for its support through the Department of Tourism, Culture and Heritage.

Pottersfield Press
83 Leslie Road
East Lawrencetown, Nova Scotia, Canada, B2Z 1P8
Website: www.pottersfieldpress.com
To order, phone toll-free 1-800-NIMBUS9 (1-800-646-2879)
Printed in Canada

*"When you look for me,
look for me in your heart.
When I have found a new place there,
I will live in you forever."*

– Antoine de Saint-Exupéry

*"Wenn ihr mich sucht,
sucht mich in eurem Herzen.
Habe ich dort eine neue Bleibe gefunden,
lebe ich in euch weiter."*

CONTENTS

PREFACE

It has always been a favourite expression of mine that "human nature is a grand thing." I believe that people are very different in their opinions, outlooks, ideas, or just the way they view life's occurrences. We deal with events in our lives in our own ways. Probably due to my twenty or so years as a canoe and hockey coach, I have met hundreds of people. Some are still friends, some are now just acquaintances, and others have long passed out of my life. The one thing everyone I've ever known all have in common is that they are all different.

I believe that the most difficult life experience any of us will ever have to go through or deal with is the loss of a loved one, a child in particular. The natural order of life, if there indeed is one, is that parents should die before their children. The closest I had ever been to thinking that I might lose one of my children was watching my then one-and-half-year-old son suffer a febrile seizure. Not terribly alarming if you happen to know the risks of a febrile seizure but as a first for any parent, it scares the good very much out of you. I have lost both of my parents as well as both sets of grandparents and enough cousins, friends, and acquaintances to believe that I am somewhat qualified to make this assessment.

My mom died in May of 1981 at the relatively young age of thirty-nine after a brief but brutal battle with non-Hodgkin's lymphoma. In terms of hitting so close to home, this was my first real experience with death. It did, however, open the floodgates. My maternal grandfather went just months later, followed by my dad's parents, and Gran, my maternal grandmother. My dad died on December 14, 2004, only months before what would become, even with all that had preceded it, the most difficult time of my life.

I had a particularly rough time with the loss of both of my grandmothers. With my father leaving the house when I was four and my mom working two jobs for many years after, my grandmothers became the main go-tos for my two brothers and me; they were the glue that held us together. They each had their own unique way of giving but each was so important to the growing years of the three of us.

The coping mechanism I used most during those times was writing. Although I wrote a lot, it was poetry that I seemed to play with the most. Writing just seemed to be a comfortable way of putting my thoughts together and trying to make sense of things. Writing was always for my own personal comfort. I'm sure fewer than ten people have read anything that I've ever written. I always wrote just to make myself feel a little better when I was feeling down.

With the death of my stepdaughter, Tiffany, I picked up a pencil again. (This is the only time I will refer to

Tiff as my stepdaughter. She became my daughter from the moment she and her mother entered my life. Tiffany was not yet two.) I started to, and still do, write to Tiff in a journal and I find comfort there.

I also found myself reading more and more. Mostly I would read anything I could find that gave me insight into how others dealt with the loss of a loved one, their children in particular. I did actually find some comfort in the knowledge that Lisa and I were not alone with our anguish. Truly, and I know that the words would never be enough to describe it, unless you are a parent who has lost a child at a too young age, then life remains fairly routine.

I think people have been surprised when they haven't seen Lisa and me sprawled and wallowing on the floor. The reality is that no one sees Lisa waking in the middle of the night after a bad dream or not having the strength to lift herself out of bed every day. No one has seen Emma crying herself to sleep night after night. And nobody is sitting with me in Tiff's room until all hours asking her to try to find her way home. Alone time in our home is, even now, complete devastation.

Tiffany's death has provoked the most intense pain and anguish we will ever fight through. Others out there have dealt, and are still dealing, with that same pain. It crept into my thoughts that if reading the stories of how others have dealt with the death of their own children (not just the grief after the death itself but the events leading to the loss) has helped me, then perhaps knowing what our family has endured might help others, if only to know that they are not alone. So that is one of the reasons for my writing this book. But only one.

From the moment we received that awful telephone call on that February day in 2006, support for our family has been plentiful. There are many, many people in our community who have shown they genuinely care for the well-being of our family but who also would like to know what happened on that day and in the weeks that followed. Again, it goes to that human nature thing.

Tiffany's story has been told over and over in the media and often with jumbled facts. Losing Tiffany was the most difficult, but simultaneously memorable, time in my life. Anyone who was near our family during our ordeal is a part of that. Any of those who helped us through, in any way, will always have a foremost place in my heart. It's one of the reasons I could never see myself moving away from this community where I live. I thought it fair that our family get what really happened out to those people who care.

I think back on the day my mom died, an overcast and damp Saturday morning in May of 1981. My grandmother sat in a chair in the corner of our living room and rocked back and forth. She rocked for the longest time. Nothing we could say or do could console her. Her pain was so much more intense than mine but I didn't understand why. After all, it was my mom who had died. On March 8 of 2006, I got it. I understood why. So to Gran, if you happen to be standing at my shoulder as I write, *I get it.*

Perhaps lastly, I still find therapy in writing. When we really sit and think about it, our thoughts and words are all we really have. Nothing else is really permanent. Truthfully, I don't know if this book will ever be read by more than twenty people, but I do know I will be one of that twenty. Perhaps that is all of the reason for writing.

Many of the days and events that took place after we received that first telephone call are still obscured by grief, worry, both mental and physical exhaustion, and even guilt among many other emotions. Some of the events are still cloudy and I may not remember them in exact detail. For example, there are definitely some days on the banks of the canal when I really don't know how long I may have sat in a spot, or how far I walked. Other things, I remember vividly and sometimes, I think, too vividly. I know the path I have taken, just not every place I have put my foot.

So the following is that story. Our true story of trying to find any kind of inner peace after losing our most precious treasure ... our daughter.

TIFFANY IS MISSING

Tiffany's first road race came at age five, a local Natal Day run. She ran the entire two-mile course without stopping.

In the early afternoon on any clear February day, the kitchen of our Dartmouth, Nova Scotia, home is bright and flooded with sunlight. Sunday the 19th, 2006, was exactly that kind of day, brilliant and bright with just a hint of winter chill outside. We had only been in our new home for a few months and were still a bit giddy over our good fortune. We had found a home in our favourite neighbourhood of the city, located on a private, dead-end street with a beautiful green and a small lake directly across the street. Life was coming together for us. Lisa, my wife, had been working at her career with an actuarial consulting firm for more than fifteen years and I as a carpenter. The two incomes gave us enough to live comfortably and enable us to do the things for our children that I was unable to do through my growing years.

For Lisa and me, it was our children that gave us our absolute joy. We had three beautiful children. Emma, who had just turned eleven, is the artsy member of our family and cares about everyone and everything. I've often said that Emma has more compassion and more kindness to give than any child I've ever been around. Derek, then thirteen, is athletic, a good student and extraordinarily charismatic.

Much of our thought in these days, however, had been centred on our twenty-year-old daughter, Tiffany. Tiffy had been working as an au pair in the northern German city of Hamm since the previous June. She had actually lucked into this opportunity shortly after finishing a year-long work term at a stable a couple of hours outside of Dartmouth. Actually, that might be overstating it, if only a litte bit. Hamm is a not-so-exciting industrial city located on the Lippe River. The Datteln-Hamm shipping canal begins its forty-kilometre trek in Datteln and then runs through Hamm, parallel to the Lippe. Hamm's only tourist draws actually reside in the historic cities and towns, such as Dortmund and Münster, not far away. Tiffany's godmother had a friend whose daughter was returning from the au pair position in Hamm. When the German family began looking for an English-speaking replacement, Tiffany jumped on it.

That Sunday morning began not much differently than any other. After a breakfast together, Emma left the house to meet with a few of her school buddies, leaving Lisa to fend for herself against relentless teasing from Derek and me. I don't recall now what prompted our hazing of Lisa but I do know the lightness of the mood was shattered moments later.

When the telephone rang just after 1:20 p.m., we assumed it was one of Lisa's sisters calling to confirm plans for our great-nephew's baptism later that afternoon. Lisa picked up the phone as Derek and I continued to trade barbs. I do not recall now whether Lisa actually spoke any words or if it was just a low and panicked sob. I do remember turning to see her, white and shaking, and unable to hold on to the telephone. She told whoever was on the other end to "please speak to my husband," though she never actually handed me the receiver. As I took the phone from Lisa's now trembling hands, the only thing that Lisa could manage was "Tiffany is missing."

From that exact moment forward, our lives changed forever. Everything we will ever do, think, and the ways in which we interact ... nothing will ever be the same.

Willem Buerger-Sturm, Tiffany's employer and acting dad in Germany, was on the other end of the phone. It was obvious, even through the phone, that Willem was struggling to find words. "This is Willem calling from Hamm. I'm sorry but I must tell you that Tiffany is missing. We did not know how long we should wait to call you."

I didn't understand at first. What did he mean? Missing? Was she late coming back from the mall? Out with friends?

Willem told me that Tiffany had been paddling with her training group on the canal where her kayak club was located. She fell behind the group on the way back to the club during the cool-down after her workout. "She paddled beneath a bridge not far from the clubhouse but never came out the other side. The coach found her boat on shore but we have not found Tiffany."

15

Willem continued on with what he knew to that point. "The police are conducting a land search in the area. They believe perhaps she may have gotten out of the boat to talk to a friend or maybe go to the store."

My mind began to race. Why did they need the police? How long had Tiff been missing?

I tried, even so far away and without all the facts, to search for the best scenario. Her boat, a K1, was on the shore … that was a good sign. She couldn't be in the water then. I don't know if it was the tone in Willem's voice or just instinct, but even as I was creating the best outcome in my head, I feared the worst. As a family, we had faced crisis before. It was different this time.

Willem had been silent on the other end of the phone.

"What else can you tell me?" My fear was growing.

His reply was almost apologetic. "The authorities also believe that she may be in the water. The water police and fire department in Hamm have been searching the water for a few hours … I am so sorry."

I couldn't breathe. I was stunned. I was again searching for, I don't know, something positive. I had to find a way to change this. It didn't seem real. Tiff was okay. She had to be. What did I have to do to change Willem's words? Lisa and Derek had remained in the kitchen through my conversation to this point. Lisa was struggling badly and D had no idea what was happening or how to make things better for his mom.

I don't know if I hesitated to ask Willem the next question because I didn't want Lisa to hear it or because I didn't want to know myself. "How cold is the water there now?"

Lisa reacted to the question before Willem did: just a cold and distraught "Oh no." There was again a hesitation on Willem's end. I could sense that as far as he was concerned, any news was bad news at this point.

"The water is three or four degrees. The coaches first noticed that she was missing about five hours ago. Kevin, the area is very small. I find it inconceivable that if she has fallen in the water she could not have gotten to the land."

Lisa was in quite a bad state at this point and I thought she might pass out. I asked Willem to call back the very moment he learned anything new or I would call him for more details. I had to try to calm Lisa. It was very early, obviously too early, to start giving up hope. Tiff was probably fine, sitting in an Internet café nearby. It was just a misunderstanding. As reassuring as I was trying to be, I think my own fears were seeping through.

Lisa was just hurting. I asked Derek to take his mother to the family room and sit with her. I realize now that was unfair. He was not equipped to handle that. He was young and didn't really understand what was going on.

I couldn't deal with both situations and needed help. Hoping they had not yet left for the church, I called Lisa's sister Joanne and her husband Keith. "Can you come over here right away? Tiffany is missing and I need someone to be with Lisa so I can find out what exactly is going on."

I believe I was thinking a little more clearly by this point and this lulled me into what proved to be a false sense that everything would be fine. Even though we didn't have all the facts, I was starting to really believe that the phone would ring at any moment to say Tiff had turned up and was fine.

I sat with Lisa and Derek until Joanne and Keith arrived ten or fifteen minutes later. I could only tell them what I knew to that point. They stayed with Lisa in the family room while I called Willem back for more, or more recent, information.

"There is nothing new. We are waiting to hear from the police as well." Willem kept insisting that the canal was too narrow, that even if Tiff had gone in the water, she would have been able to get to the shore. Again, I asked him to please call with any information, no matter how trivial.

The moment I hung up the phone, I knew we had to get to Germany. Bad news, good news, it didn't matter. We had to be there with Tiffany. I needed to see her and hold her. Lisa had been thinking the same thing. She came into the kitchen as I hung up and we said almost in unison, "We have to go to Hamm." After explaining our circumstance to the airline, they were very helpful and did their best to accommodate us.

We were still not able to get out of Halifax on a flight to Frankfurt until the next afternoon. I remember trying to think of any way to get there sooner but no other option existed. All we could do was sit and wait.

Throughout the day, we received bits and pieces of information. One report, from the Hamm police via Willem, had both Tiffany and her kayak being seen on the shore. Another had someone calling to her from a bridge. I know that Lisa was sinking further into worry as the hours went by but I was trying to remain optimistic. The more time that passed, however, the more difficult it was to hold on to that feeling.

Willem called again. Apparently, there had been more than one report of a young woman being seen on the shore of the canal near the spot where Tiff's empty boat was found. "The police are searching more on land. They think that perhaps she has run away … or perhaps was kidnapped."

I was immediately suspicious of both of these scenarios. There was no way on this earth that Tiff had run away. I was not naïve, I just knew my daughter. Tiff loved her family and was loved by her family. She had more love and support than most and was very aware of that fact. I was more certain that Tiff would never do that to her mother. They had been through far too much together and their love for each other was endless, and remains that way even now.

So as far as the theory of a kidnapping went, I found it hard to fathom that she could have been kidnapped from her boat, in the canal, in the middle of the day. Did a person she knew call her to the shore and once there had she been taken against her will?

I didn't know which nightmare was worse. Was she in the water, or had someone actually been able to lure her to the shore and take her away and was hurting her now? It truly was torture either way.

Someone mentioned that maybe she was lost. It was dark now in Hamm and Lisa fell deeper into her despair. "Tiffany is afraid of the dark." She would have been wet with not enough clothes to keep her warm. We were so afraid for her and wanted desperately to be there for her, to hold her and comfort her. But we were frozen miles and miles away with no way to reach her.

More of the family arrived as the day went on, obviously aware that something was very wrong when we, and Joanne and Keith, failed to show at the church. As the family became more aware of the circumstance, the overall feeling became more one of doom.

Even though things looked so bleak, I tried my best to present a feeling of optimism. We knew nothing for certain and we had to keep hoping for the best. None of us really knew what to do. We wandered from room to room or just stared at the floor, waiting for any type of good news from Germany.

I remember calling the RCMP. I didn't know what they could possibly do but I knew it couldn't hurt. The officer I spoke with confirmed their own helplessness but did wonder, to me, if she had contacted any of her friends here at home. I tried a few of Tiffany's closer friends but to no avail. They had not heard from Tiff for days.

It was late Sunday evening now and Tiffany had been missing in Germany for almost fifteen hours without any sign. I was more desperate than ever and felt absolute helplessness being on this side of the ocean. What was being done in Hamm? Were the police still searching? I wondered if they had gotten her picture out to the community or if that was something we should do. I called a good friend at our local newspaper; perhaps he could get Tiffany's picture and information to the local newspapers in Hamm. George asked me to e-mail Tiffany's picture and whatever else was needed, along with the address information for the local German papers, and he would do his best.

Lisa called Kattia, Tiffany's house-mother and employer, to get this information. It was during that telephone conversation that some of the facts surrounding

Tiff's disappearance were made clearer and it was then that our hopes of Tiffany being found alive began to destruct.

Tiffany's boat had not been found on the shore of the canal, as we had first been told. It was in fact found floating in the canal. Her kayak paddle was found in the water just a few metres away. I have been involved with sprint kayaks for almost forty years. I knew things, even here, that the authorities in Hamm did not know. I knew Tiffany … and I knew that she was gone. Lisa knew it as well.

Until Tiffany was found, we knew we had to, and would, carry on with a search. There still was the faintest hope she was still out there somewhere, and I knew I would never, ever give up on my child, but in our hearts Lisa and I both knew. I remember thinking, actually hoping now, that she had really been kidnapped. Under that circumstance, she was at least still alive and I would still get to her. As I reviewed what we knew already, though, reality kicked in again and I began to realize we were hoping against all hope.

Someone had suggested we should get hold of a German friend of ours, Christine Hoehne, to help with the translations with the German authorities. It would be light again in Hamm in a few hours and the police would be continuing their search. We were anxious to know what they were doing and perhaps they could tell us more than the Sturms did.

I told Christine what had happened, or what we knew, to that point. She was entertaining a church group but would find out what she could and call me back. She did call back – I think around 11:00 p.m. – to tell me she had found a news article about the day's events in a German newspaper online. Her voice and tone were somber and I knew the article was not good.

When she asked, "Are you sure that you want me to read this?" I remember remarking that I don't think she could tell us anything we did not already know. As Christine read the article, there indeed were no surprises … until she came to the end of the article when she paused.

"Kevin," she asked, "do you want me to continue?"

I couldn't think of how things could be any worse. "Please finish."

Christine finished the last sentence: "German officials fear the worst."

I sat numb and speechless for a few moments and Christine let me gather myself. This was further confirmation to us that Tiffany was in the water. Christine offered to come to our house at around 2:30 a.m., when the day was just beginning in Hamm, to make any calls to the German authorities that we might require.

Christine Hoehne has been one of several friends who have been absolutely amazing for us as we have gone through our struggles. She has been our translator on many different levels: with the police and water officials in Germany, the newspapers in Hamm as well as any other purpose. She was even able, with the help of her physician father, to have Tiffany's autopsy report translated later. While this may seem odd to some, it was important for Lisa and me to learn as many of the facts surrounding Tiffany's death as we could. Knowing all we could, we thought, would help us with any eventual healing.

Christine came to our house at 2:00 a.m. on Monday morning. She had learned little else from any of the other German newspapers. We had sent pictures of Tiffany earlier on Sunday evening, and they were being published.

Until she was found, Tiff's disappearance was still being treated as a "missing person" case.

We had Christine call Willem first. Perhaps there had been some more news? At first Willem was very skeptical of speaking with anyone, fearing it was some "bad" media. Once feeling safe he reported no new information. He only repeated that it was beyond rational that Tiff could not get to shore. "The area is so small, she could not have been more than fifteen feet from the land," he insisted. I can remember thinking it didn't really matter how far from the shore she was; Tiff was missing and that is what we had to deal with.

Willem gave us the telephone number for the water police in Datteln-Hamm who were coordinating the search. It took a couple of tries before we were able to get through to anyone. When we did, the entire conversation was in German and this only added to the feeling of helplessness Lisa and I already had.

The authorities were still following up on the reports that a young woman wearing red clothing had been seen near the place where Tiffany had last been seen in her boat. They did not, however, feel that there was great validity in these reports and their belief was that Tiffany was in the water and that she would not be found alive. Still, the search both in the canal as well as on land had resumed at first light. These were things we already knew.

On hanging up the telephone, Christine was confident that the authorities were doing all they could do and we believed they were, but I think Lisa and I were both too emotionally exhausted to comprehend much more of anything at that point. Up to that stage, this had already been the most difficult day of our married lives. It was going to get so much worse. Lisa went upstairs to try to get some rest before leaving for Germany later that day.

I remember sitting in the kitchen for what could have been minutes or hours. I was again hoping against all hope that the phone would ring, that our Tiffy would be on the other end telling us she was okay, that she wanted to come home to be with us. But I knew then it was now very unlikely and that it was one call we would never receive again.

When the phone did ring, sometime around mid-morning, it was a member of the local print media. Apparently, the story had been picked up from the newspapers in Hamm. I was asked if I would consent to an interview or had any new information to offer. The more time that passed, the bigger the story got and the farther away Tiffany got. I couldn't think. I believe I told the gentleman on the other end of the line that I really didn't know much more than he did and I had nothing more to offer.

The fact that the press was now calling scared me. It was even more confirmation that all this was really happening. I don't recall who, if anyone, suggested that we use the press to our advantage. This was a way to get word out to Tiff's friends to let them know she was missing and that if she was in touch, to call us. When the television news called a short time later, I accepted the interview opportunity. I was well aware, however, that my emotional state would not get me through any kind of question and answer session on camera. We needed someone to look after any press, not just for that day but in the days to come. We were leaving for Germany in just a few hours. Our family would no doubt have to deal with the media while we were gone. I certainly wanted Derek and Emma to be kept away from any upsetting situations.

A brother-in-law, Darrell Fraser, agreed to appear on camera that day. Darrell is a man of integrity and honesty and has always presented an air of calmness. He is also Tiffany's godfather and I knew this would be an incredibly difficult thing for him. But I also knew for certain that he would represent Tiff well. Lisa has a very close family and they, all of them, have been a solid wall of support. Again, there was never any question that Darrell would represent our family well. He did just that. During that first interview in our living room, we only presented what we knew to be true regarding Tiffany's disappearance and we asked if anyone had heard from Tiffany that they please call us. Any communication between our family and the press after that morning fell to Darrell and other members of our family. Lisa and I had little awareness of the scale the story would reach at home for weeks afterwards.

Saying goodbye to D and Em late that morning was difficult on so many levels. We would be away from them when they were going to need us most. What type of media circus were we leaving them with? How long would we be away from them? The worst thought of all was knowing that we were leaving them and when we did come home, we would most likely be bringing Tiffany home to them in a casket.

I honestly do not remember now how we travelled to the airport. I do know there were media there. I ran into a friend who works at Air Canada and from the very moment I told Brad Murray about Tiff's disappearance, he looked after us. Up until the time we landed in Halifax with Tiffany weeks later, Brad and the concierge staff in

Halifax, Toronto, Montreal, Frankfurt, London, wherever, were wonderful, meeting us at every landing, upgrading us to first class whenever possible, escorting us to VIP areas and back to airplanes through all of our travels. Our situation was grim but may have been made so much more unbearable if we had had to do these things on our own.

The entire trip, including the flight and subsequent car ride to the home of Willem and Kattia, would take about fifteen hours. Lisa and I sat next to each other through the entire journey but said little. I wanted so badly to take Lisa's pain from her, to tell her things would be all right. I even managed to find a way, only briefly, to believe that when we arrived in Hamm, Tiff would be there to meet us. I spent most of the flight time, naturally, thinking of Tiffany. Most of those thoughts were of recent life, things we had done together within the last year or so.

Tiff was home for almost a month over the Christmas holidays and we spent some nice time together. We worked out and ran together a bit, which was a nice by-product of her having rediscovered sprint kayaking after a couple of years away from the sport. We talked quite a bit, more than in the recent past, and caught up on life. Tiff had been thinking about staying in Germany after her work term with the Sturms ended. She was really enjoying her time overseas. I think she was really learning to enjoy her independence. This was so different from her attitude the previous June when Tiff and I travelled together in Europe for a week before she started with the Sturms. We saw the sights in Munich, Prague, the Nazi prison camp at Dachau, and the old village of Rothenberg

WHEN YOU LOOK FOR ME – KEVIN BONANG

ob der Tauber before driving to Hamm to meet Willem, Kattia, Anna, Franz, and Birgit.

I remembered Tiff's first night at the Sturms' home. I stayed at a small hotel in town while Tiff spent her first night with her new family. I went for a long walk on my own that night. I became fairly uptight during that walk thinking about leaving Tiff. This was the start of something very new for her. I was aware that the next time Tiffy came home to Dartmouth, she would be a very different young woman from the little girl Lisa and I had raised.

I thought quite a bit about our conversation the next day when I left her with the Sturms. We went for a long walk together. Tiffany confessed to me that she was really scared and didn't know what to expect or how she would do being so far from us.

I remember telling my daughter that at first she would be homesick and a bit lonely, but it would pass and then she would get on with her great life adventure. I also remember, very vividly, that when I hugged her goodbye, I did not want to let go. I was so proud of her but afraid for her at the same time.

It was incredibly hard to leave her then, but it was an amazing opportunity and this life experience would be huge for her. I remembered my own time thumbing around Europe, mostly in the north, during the winter of 1986-87 and that I learned more about myself during those months than at any other time in my life. Tiffany, I was sure, would reap those same benefits.

I thought back to Tiffany's leaving us at the airport only one month before. She was excited to be going back to her new life and friends. Again, as I hugged her goodbye, I was so proud of her. But this time it was because she had grown to be such a mature and confident young woman.

Lisa and I watched her through the gates as long as we could that day. I remember standing on a set of stairs, trying to keep her in sight as long as we could before she disappeared through the security gate. We could never have known then that was to be the last time we would see her.

ARRIVING IN HAMM, GERMANY

When Tiffany was a toddler, perhaps age two, she had these pudgy little arms and legs that gave her the look of a body builder. From this she gained the "Ah-nold" nickname.

I don't remember if it was exhaustion, wishful thinking, or if I maybe even actually believed it, but it really was in my mind that Tiffany would be at the Sturms', waiting for us when we arrived there. I wasn't sure how that could happen or under what scenario this would have taken place, but I think I actually pictured our meeting in my mind. These were among my thoughts as we travelled along the autobahn toward Hamm as Willem had the forethought to send a car service to meet Lisa and me in Frankfurt. Actually, this consumed me for most of the drive. Due to our travel time, Lisa and I had heard nothing of our daughter's fate. Maybe no news was good news? … I didn't know. It was still a dream.

I spent the rest of the three-hour driving time thinking back to Tiff's younger years and our time together then. I watched her kayak and war-canoe races again in my mind. I saw her spinning circles on our backyard rink, performing her gymnastics routines at the club where she trained years earlier, and as a Highland dancer at the Royal Nova Scotia International Tattoo. And I watched Tiff ride her horses. Being in the stable, around horses, was her passion. I wanted so badly, and always will, to go back to that time. Tiff's innocence and naivety during her growing years was truly charming. She was always fun to be around and her smile was, and still is, contagious.

There was, of course, no good news when we arrived at the Sturms' home in Hamm. As a matter of fact, there was no news at all. We learned that the authorities were still searching both land and water. Kattia had made an appointment for later in the day to meet with the detectives of the Hamm police department who were in charge of investigating Tiffany's disappearance.

The time of day was unimportant to us now. We had no idea what time of day it was or even what day of the week it was (a condition that would exist for another few months), but Kattia informed Lisa and me that we had a bit of time to gather ourselves before heading into the city.

Rather than trying to rest, we instead went to Tiff's room just to look at her things. Although we never said it to each other, and I don't think that either Lisa or I could describe it, we both felt something being around Tiff's things. I can't say it made us feel better or that being there comforted us. We just needed to be there. We looked through her clothes, glanced at some of her journal writings trying, even then, to respect her privacy but at the same time wanting to find some clue as to where she might be. "I will never give up on my child," I remember thinking.

A few hours later, Willem and Kattia took us to lunch at a very small restaurant in the city before going to speak with the police. I could not understand why we were doing this. Why were we eating when we should be out looking for Tiff? I guess Willem and Kattia knew that we had to eat to stay strong, even if Lisa and I didn't recognize it, or even care. We didn't eat, though, just picked at our food and I do not remember anything of what we spoke about. It was just uncomfortable and it was not where we wanted to be.

As we left the restaurant, a helicopter circled overhead. Willem told us then that the police had been conducting an air search for Tiffany over the canal since the time she went missing, a statement that caused my blood to run even colder. The choking fog we were in was unfortunately beginning to clear a bit more.

When we arrived at the police department, we were escorted to a room on the third floor of the building, where we sat down with four or five detectives. The room was very plain, just a large white room cluttered with chairs, a few tables and shelves. It actually would have mattered very little whether Lisa and I were in the room or not. The detectives seemed to focus on Willem and Kattia and there was very little English being spoken. Kattia and Willem did their best to ask the questions that Lisa and I needed answers to.

The Sturms truly are an amazing couple. Willem is a very intelligent and capable man when it comes to dealing with such people, not excitable by any means. He once referred to himself in a moment of jest as a "thoroughly modern man." Kattia is a bit more direct. If she doesn't get the answers she needs or thinks that perhaps she is being led astray, she will impose her will and I've learned that for her, there is no surrender. As much as Kattia can be strong-willed, however, she is also one of the most compassionate women I've ever encountered. She and I have spent our time crying together. Kattia, I know, had grown very fond of Tiffany and this ordeal was taking a toll on her as well.

There were no new developments. There were a few theories but really nothing that had any substance. The police were following leads that Tiffany had been seen in various parts of the city. One report had a witness saying they had seen a young woman standing next to a boat, under the bridge, on the previous day. There had been another report that someone had seen a young woman wearing wet clothing on the previous day at a location that would be halfway between the canal and the Sturm home.

We discussed the possibilities that maybe Tiff had run away or perhaps had gotten out of her kayak to meet someone on shore. They told us that in cases such as this, the "missing" person sometimes returns to the scene and becomes embarrassed or overwhelmed by all of the fuss they have created and will instead make their way home. They suggested this would be common behaviour for a person of Tiff's age and usually culminates in three or four days. Due to this information, there was still a heavy land search being carried out. Even as they were relaying these thoughts, however, I could sense they really didn't believe any of it themselves.

While these theories were being tossed about, one of the detectives, Johan Bosch, left the room. When he re-turned, he placed a black ball hat on the table in front of us. This hat had the word "Canada" on the front and we knew it immediately to be Tiff's. Through broken English, we learned the hat had been found just three hours before by a citizen while walking along the banks of the canal. It was floating not more than two hundred metres from where Tiffany was believed to have fallen in.

Kattia did her best to convince Lisa and me that this did not mean Tiffany was in the water. Lisa was not looking at anyone in particular when she stated that she knew Tiffany would never have run away and that she believed Tiffany really was in the water. There was no response. Again, even if nobody wanted to say it, we all knew exactly what we were dealing with. Lisa and I listened as the police explained to Willem and Kattia what their intentions were for the coming days but again, it meant little. We left the police department with their promise to call us the moment they learned anything new.

From the police department, we drove to the boathouse from where Tiff paddled to speak with Tiffany's coach, Gabriel. I'll admit now that I was not a fan of this man from the start. He just seemed to want to distance himself from the situation. Even during much of our conversation with him, he avoided looking at Lisa or me, instead focusing on Kattia and Willem.

He took us to where they had found Tiff's boat and blade about two hundred metres up the canal from the club but other than that, told us that he couldn't remember anything. I know that I wanted to grab him and shake him.

How could he not remember? How could he let this happen? Why wasn't he with her? How can you have a group on five-degree water and not have a motor boat with them? Surely, it could not be common practice to have his athletes on the water in such cold weather without PFDs (personal flotation devices) and a motor boat? These were questions that did not get answered, and really, it didn't matter at this point. Our situation was what it was. He did show us the boat Tiffany had been using. I examined the deck and hull, wondering if maybe there was damage from an object being dropped on Tiff as she was paddling under the bridge.

The only thing Gabriel could tell us for sure was a fisherman had alerted some of the athletes who were at the boathouse that there was an empty kayak floating up by the bridge. Gabriel told us he ran to that spot, retrieved the boat and paddle, and then ran to a service station not far away to call for help. The water search began immediately.

Few of the athletes at the club could remember anything definite either: not what Tiffany was wearing, whether she was wearing a hat, or where exactly they had seen her last. One young lady finally came to us to tell us that Tiffany was wearing a red top and hat. We did learn that Tiff had been paddling in a group with four or five others only minutes before she disappeared. Lisa and I were also made to understand that there had been no other traffic (such as barges) on the canal in the moments before Tiffany's disappearance.

The group apparently went on ahead while Tiff stayed back. One young man did recall paddling by Tiff in the opposite direction about two hundred metres from the bridge and said that she looked fine. This young man would be the last person to have seen Tiffany alive. From where he said that he had passed Tiffany to where she went in, Tiffany would be dead less than one minute later.

The Search

Tiff's official record for time in the shower, water running and under the spray, is actually over forty-three minutes.

Both Lisa and I grew up with the sport of sprint canoe/kayak. We did know things about the sport that the police, the water police, the fire department, or any of the Hamm authorities could not know. Staying afloat in a sprint kayak is a lot like balancing on a basketball in the water. It is conceivable that a short lapse in concentration or fatigue combined with some untimely wash can cause even the best to leave their boat.

Is this what happened to our Tiffany? Was it just a fluke and bad luck that was the cause of this tragedy? It was becoming increasingly difficult to try to hang on to that last glimmer. Until we had Tiffany home, one way or the other, there would always be a hint of hope at the back of our minds. "I will never give up on my child." It is a parent's duty to hang on to the best hopes for their children, no matter what the facts suggest.

The fact was, however, Lisa and I did know where Tiffany was. I think we did express our hopes to each other as a maybe. I don't think we ever fully conceded the worst until sixteen days later. We spent a few hours that day just walking up and down the shores of the canal, as we would do in the following days, quietly hoping for some sign of Tiffany. She was there, somewhere – we just couldn't find her. Lisa and I wanted so desperately to be the ones to find her. Nobody could love Tiff like we did. Nobody else, we thought, would bring her gently out of the cold water. No one else would wrap Tiff in a blanket to hold her and make her warm, or brush her beautiful hair. These are things that only a parent could want for their child.

Lisa and I were back the next morning to walk the shores again, back and forth all day in the miserable cold. Much of our time in the following days was the same, just walking and looking. Sometimes we spoke and sometimes we just walked alone with our thoughts. Every once in a while, a boat from the water police would pass by on their search. Lisa and I would stop and watch them go by, wondering if they had anything they could tell us. The officers on board knew, of course, exactly who we were. They would only look back at us with glum faces. We understood that they too were hurting. I think they wanted to find our little girl almost as desperately as we did.

Lisa and I started back to the Sturms' home well after dark on that first day. We were very unsure of directions and as it happened, one of the athletes Tiffany had been paddling with the day before offered to lead part of the way for us. At the turn where we were to separate, he got out of his car and walked back to us. I got out of the car to meet him and listened as this young fellow, in broken English, tried to express just how badly he felt about all that had happened. He told me the best way he could that Tiffany had been so well received and admired by the other athletes at the club, that she had become a real friend to everyone. Although this made me feel good, if only for a moment, I got the strangest feeling this lad knew more than he was letting on. I don't, even for a moment, believe now that this was anything but a terrible accident, but I still wish I had been able to spend more time with him.

Because we had been so focused on Tiffany, we were unaware of anything that had been happening at home in Dartmouth. We were getting some information from Lisa's family, but mostly, conversations centred on our progress and how or if we were holding it together. I cannot recall now which day it might have been but on one of the early days we received a telephone call from Don Shewfelt.

Don and his wife, Donna, have been two of those friends who have been so good to us. They, along with good friend David MacDonald, had been largely responsible for a fundraising campaign (one that Lisa and I knew nothing about until days later) that would later help us to pay for expenses going back and forth to Germany and our expenses there.

Don was calling more to let us know that if we needed anything at all from our community at home, everyone was anxious to do anything they could. Donna later told us it was difficult for many of our friends and acquaintances to imagine what Lisa and I had been going through. If they couldn't be with us to hold our hands as we searched, then helping with the costs was something they could do. I have said this to anyone who will listen over the months since: we are so grateful to our community for the way they have supported and held us up during and since Tiffany's death.

Don also told me that day my two youngest children had been nothing but courageous over the days that Lisa and I had been gone. He told me Derek had continued to play hockey and had become a team leader and that he couldn't have been more proud of D. I could really tell that Don was having a rough time holding it together, which was causing me to fall apart. I handed the phone to Lisa and went for a short walk.

By Wednesday evening, Lisa and I were as beaten down as parents could be. The emotional torment combined with the physical exhaustion of travel and long days of searching in the cold and not eating very much had left us both pretty much on the brink of collapse. Willem and Kattia fed us well that night, including more wine than we perhaps should have had. Probably a good thing. Lisa and I were both in desperate need of rest and sleep, no matter how it was brought on.

We were up early the next morning, though (Thursday, February 23), and on our way to the canal. Our routine over those few days was to park the Sturms' Smart car in the clubhouse parking lot and start our search from there. On this morning, however, the police had the main driveway to the clubhouse blocked off. Lisa and I didn't have to wonder for very long just what was happening. The police immediately waved us through to the club and as we approached the activity, one police officer came toward the car to intercept us.

This officer, Marcus Tiemann, would turn out to be a blessing for us, not only on that day but in the weeks and even months to come. I think Marcus ended up on that assignment on that day mostly because he spoke some degree of English. I would also figure out later that Marcus was really not cut out to do this type of police work. He struggled with us through every difficult moment Lisa and I would endure, far too compassionate to put himself through this, I thought. It was that very attribute, however, that caused Marcus to fight for us, to have the search continue in future days even when those in authority above him thought otherwise. He and I seem to share the same outlook on life and we both adore our children (he has a little boy, five years old at the time). Marcus did leave this line of police work shortly after Tiffany was found, but I am glad to say he remains my good friend today.

There had been some talk about bringing in "cadaver" dogs to help with the search. These dogs, we were told, had the special ability to scent out human flesh on or just below the surface of the water. Lisa and I agreed, of course, to use the dogs as we were desperate to try anything. Three dogs were there that day and for that moment, we were pinning our hopes on these animals.

Lisa and I watched from a cold bench by the canal as the dogs came and went. At one point, I got up to go to the car to retrieve my gloves, but the police around us quickly intervened and asked me not to go back to the car as the "bad" press had begun to gather and would show me no mercy. In the coming days, photos of Lisa and me, taken from a distance, would turn up in a German version of the *National Enquirer*. It would not be my last encounter with the "bad" press. The idea of interaction with these people actually appealed to me at that point but Marcus was adamant, handed me his gloves and asked me to please stay put.

As we continued to watch for what I think was just about an hour or so, we realized that each dog had begun to return in a frenzy from their separate excursion on the water. Marcus then came to us and explained that each dog had picked up a scent in the same location on the canal. They had done this separately so there was no chance that the dogs could only be reacting to each other. Divers were being called in immediately.

I remember Marcus looking at me and asking if I thought I was going to be sick. Actually, I had no idea what I felt ... or if I felt. I knew that Lisa and I had to be close if the divers did, in fact, find Tiffany. He took us to a place where we could both watch the divers search and the press could be kept away. We were told it might be a few hours before anything happened so Lisa and I sat in the Smart car to stay warm and to wait.

I had never been comfortable with the idea of Lisa seeing Tiffany if she was brought out of the water and thought it best to talk about it before we were faced with that situation. I was fully aware that Lisa wanted desperately to be able to hold Tiff, no matter what. All I could think about was Lisa's last memory of her baby being less than perfect. Lisa was too weak and distraught to argue, I think, so we agreed that if Tiffany was brought out of the water on that day, then I would be there. I promised to wrap her in a blanket, brush her hair, and do all of those things we had talked about.

Lisa and I waited for hours, just watching and hoping. We did doze off a bit, I think, but for the most part we just waited. I got out of the car from time to time to speak with Marcus, to find out if they were getting any closer.

"They have found nothing but are flying in sonar equipment from Dortmund to help locate larger objects on the bottom of the canal."

It was getting late in the day and I wondered if it might be getting too late and our opportunity was slipping away. It was also getting colder and as Marcus hunched his shoulders against that cold, I thanked him for his diligence. He shared that he was amazed at how much courage Lisa and I were showing. The comment confused me. I hadn't considered my actions or reactions one way or the other, I was just reacting.

I went back to the car to sit with Lisa. As I sat back in my seat, Lisa reached over and put her hand on mine. She thanked me for "being her rock" and being the one to deal with the police and speak to the authorities. More confusion. What else should I be doing? I did understand that Lisa was being supportive and her intent was to let me know that she was grateful for my doing the things she was just not up to. I think she also realized just how important Tiffany was to me. When it came to parenting our children, Lisa and Tiffany always, for obvious reasons, have had a very close bond with each other. Although I did and always will envy that relationship, I made it a point to let Lisa do most of the parenting when it came to Tiff. Because of this, I often wonder these days if Tiffy really knew how important she was in my life and how thankful I was to her for what she had also taught me.

During the day, we watched over forty divers repeat the same process: go in the water, come out to get warm in the mobile units and then go back in. At one point, a priest came by to speak with us but really didn't say much. He spent much of his time with the police. Again, a language thing, I think. Kattia came late in the day to bring us tea and some food.

We were told this search had now become the most massive the city of Hamm had ever conducted. We had no reason to doubt this. There were rescue vehicles, police vehicles, ambulances, divers, citizens, and media, all covering four or five blocks on the downtown side of the canal. Lisa, Marcus, the priest, I and a few others were holding vigil on the green on the other side of the canal. It was almost dark now but the divers were still going. Apparently, darkness didn't matter much because the divers couldn't see anything at the bottom anyway; they were conducting more of a search "by feel." It was more the cold that was becoming the issue.

We had also been told earlier in the day that for health and safety concerns, each diver was only permitted to go in the water twice. Marcus told us later that, even with these rules in place, every time a diver came out of the water, looked up the embankment to Lisa and me, they would go right back in, no matter how freaking cold they were. We are still very grateful to those people. Their work was truly extraordinary and they were doing this not because it was their job but because they were hurting right along with Lisa and me. We did learn that the vast majority of divers present that day were there of their own accord, off the clock.

There did come a point, however, when Lisa, Kattia, Marcus, the chief of the fire department, and I had to give up for the night. Just ten or so hours before, we thought for certain we would have Tiffany back and at least a start to some closure. But it was not to happen on that day.

We drove back to the Sturms' in silence, darkness and pain. We knew that our sweet girl was in that canal, somewhere. Our level of desperation continued to increase. I still believe we were close that day. We just missed her.

My concern for Lisa, both her physical well-being and especially her emotional state, was growing by the hour. I was managing to somehow maintain some focus, or perhaps that is only my recollection now. I do know at that time, I was determined to stay the course, to search the canal for as long as it took, to be the one to find our little girl and bring her home. Lisa, however, needed to be home. I was very well aware that she was as determined as I was to be there, but she was sliding and needed more support than even I could give her. We also had two children at home in Dartmouth, who were no doubt struggling as badly as we were and needed their mom and dad. I felt guilty admitting it for the longest time, but Derek and Emma had not been on my mind much. I can justify that now by knowing they were being well looked after at home. Lisa's family is truly amazing in that regard. Although I missed D and Em greatly, Tiffy needed us now.

When two of Lisa's five sisters, Cathy and Beth, arrived the next day, in part to just support us but also to take Lisa home to Dartmouth, I was very thankful. They arrived at the Hamm rail terminal around supper time. Lisa and I walked the kilometre or so from the boathouse to the train station, Lisa's steps getting quicker as we went. That meeting was very emotional for all of us. Lisa and I were hurting and other than Willem, Kattia and their kids, we were for the most part on our own. The girls, I'm sure, recognized we were struggling and were just as glad to be there for us. After settling them at the hotel a short distance away, we returned to the canal to search some more. We filled Cathy and Beth in on all we knew, including the fact that we were certain Tiffany was in the water and the chances of finding her were growing slimmer as the hours went by. Cathy and Beth walked the canal with us for another couple of days.

Throughout our early days of the search, Lisa and I continued to hear of support from home. One friend in particular was anxious to help. I am fortunate in that I have made some good friends over the years. One of them is Angus Borland. Gus has extensive commercial diving experience, especially in finding lost items in crappy underwater conditions. The floor of the Datteln-Hamm canal is mostly just silt, and any movement from the divers or boats would stir this silt, making visibility under the water about twenty centimetres. We had heard from home that Gus was anxious to come to Hamm and help in any way he could. I had no doubt the authorities were doing all they could, but there were some things I didn't understand about the water search. I called Gus, more just to pick his brain and get his thoughts on the way the search was being conducted.

"Kevin, do you want me over there? I think I could help." I thought that was too much. Gus has a worldwide company to run and his own family to consider as well.

"I can't ask you to do that," I told him.

There was a short silence on the other end of the phone and then "Kev, I know that you would do it for me." He had me. Angus arrived in Hamm the next day.

Almost since the time that Lisa and I had arrived in Germany, Kattia and I had been trying to convince the executive of the kayak club to allow me the use of a motor boat. I thought I could cover much more distance on the water than on foot. Eventually, they agreed to get me on the water in the next days in the company of one of the club coaches.

I was somewhat hesitant to involve just anyone in such a search. What if we did find Tiff? How would just anyone react to that? I was assured they did have a fellow who was more than anxious to help and knew well what he was getting into. Alexander was completely compassionate about what we were dealing with. He made it clear from the very start that whatever I needed to do, he was in and we got out on the water five or so times in the days following.

We didn't speak much during those times. I would stay in the bow and point to where I wanted to go or if I thought an object just might be my girl. Alexander would sit at the wheel and steer. It was incredibly cold on the water. Moving into the wind brought tears to my eyes and pain to the rest of my body. Alexander remained steadfast in his promise. He was going to be out there as long as I needed him and I, in turn, felt better not being on the water alone. We arrived back at the boathouse after our first time out just as darkness was creeping in and after a particularly cold afternoon. Gus had arrived while we were on the water and was upstairs with Lisa, the girls and maybe a couple of club members. They were all sitting with Mr. Bannach, an officer with the water police. This unit of law enforcement is generally responsible for the goings-on of the Datteln-Hamm canal.

The club, one of a number, is located on a shipping canal and it is on this canal that the athletes train. So, apparently, when a shipping barge goes by, the athletes just get out of the way of the barge and its wash and hope for the best. When one considers that this canal is only thirty or so metres wide at some parts, this makes it, at the very least, a questionable practice. I remember thinking that Tiffany could not have been the only fatality these people have dealt with.

Mr. Bannach was very honest with us. Even though the police were still searching on land to some extent, the belief now was that Tiffany was, in fact, lost in the murky waters of the canal. Lisa and I were told that the canal travelled its forty kilometres or so through a series of locks before it finally terminated at a junction with another, larger, waterway. We were told that due to the currents in the canal, along with the traffic, it was possible that Tiffany's body could be taken far away from the place she actually went into the water. It could be months, or longer, before Tiffany was found. The possibility that Tiffany would never be found also existed. Lisa asked how those in other towns would know who Tiffany was if she was ever found so far away. Bannach was reassuring in this regard: "Our communications are in place. Everyone along the waterway knows of our situation."

During our conversation, we learned that Tiffany could stay under the water for anywhere between one and three weeks. Gases would have to form in her body before she would come to the surface. Mr. Bannach's expression turned almost apologetic as he told us, just before he left us, that they could not close commercial traffic on the canal indefinitely and that regular shipping on the canal would have to resume within a couple of days. I was told the canal is between twenty to twenty-four feet deep and the barges take up to sixteen feet of water. That didn't leave much room for Tiff, I thought. Lisa had been thinking the same thing. All I could do was hold her as she told me that she couldn't bear the thought of Tiffany being in the path of a ship's propeller. These were the harsh realities. The chances were very real that we would never see our little girl again. Not even to bury her.

I now had an opportunity to speak with Gus. Angus and I have never been really close but there is a strong mutual respect between us. We told Angus what we knew and I told him about the search methods I had observed while the divers were in the water. Gus explained that the grid method of search the Hamm fire department had been using was common, but not his own preferred method of crossing the canal with a line, walking the line and if nothing is found, move up a metre and cross again. This process would be repeated until there was success. He told me then he had a colleague in London who was also anxious to help and was actually readying gear to cross the Channel if we needed him.

I had no idea what to do. Commercial traffic was set to resume on the canal, which would make for obvious constant interruption in this type of search, but more to the point would make such a search almost useless. Any new traffic on the canal could move Tiffany's body to an area that had already been searched. We also had no real idea where to even start any new search. I just couldn't rationalize anything.

It was Sunday evening (February 26) and Cathy and Beth were taking Lisa back home early the next morning. Lisa and I spent the evening packing some of Tiffany's things for Lisa to take home. We spent a restless night at the Sturms' before getting up in the darkness to meet the girls at the hotel. We talked about what had to be done at home in Dartmouth. Lisa would have to call our dentist to arrange to have Tiff's dental records sent to Hamm in the event they were needed for identification in the future. She would have to be a parent to Derek and Emma the best way she could. I did know that her family would be there at every turn at home, to help and support her in anything she needed. We spoke about my staying in Hamm alone and how I would manage. I tried somewhat awkwardly to assure Lisa that I would be okay, although I honestly had no idea what the days ahead would bring.

The parting in front of the hotel was so difficult. I wanted to be with Lisa, to look after her. I was completely panicked about how she was going to cope in the days ahead. But I had also made a promise to her. I was going to stay in Hamm for as long as it took to find Tiffany and I would do all the things we had talked about when I found her. I would make her comfortable just like her mom wanted. Lisa and the girls left in the darkness of the early morning of Monday, February 27. I went to the canal to search for a couple of hours before waking Gus at the hotel.

The fire officials were agreeable to continuing the search with Angus participating, even with the obstacles that resumed commercial shipping presented. If Gus wanted to go in the water, then they were for it, anything to try to get Tiff back. After a quick trip to the police station that morning, we went to the Hamm fire department to look at their gear thinking maybe Gus could make use of it. I can safely say that this was the Taj Mahal of fire facilities. This building easily took up two city blocks with nothing but the best of equipment. They had trucks of every description, boats, all of the best gear that modern technology can provide. The German government sees to it that their rescue services want for nothing.

While at the station, we learned that one of the kayak club's athletes had noticed a foul odor while paddling by a particular area of the canal. The police were calling in the cadaver dogs again to assist with a search within an hour. Marcus drove Gus and me the short distance from the fire station to a location that was different from our first search with the dogs.

It was near a set of docks that I had become very familiar with. It was also up-current from the Münsterstrasse Bridge where Tiff had disappeared. Because of the long chain used to secure the docks from surface to bottom, and since I knew that Tiffany had been wearing a splash cover, I thought it very possible that Tiff could be tangled here somehow. It was cold and the low cloud made it very dark for the early afternoon hour. A cold wind out of the northwest added to the frigid conditions and to the height of the water.

The dogs were on the water, again, one at a time but being bounced all over the small motor boat by the choppy water conditions. I wondered how the dogs would find any scent with both the strong winds and lousy water. Still, the divers were readying themselves to go in the water regardless of what the dogs found. Apparently, they figured that since they were here anyway they would go to work.

Gus and I watched from the paddy wagon. The "bad" press were again present, unwavering in their quest to feed off the misery of others. Marcus brought us some hot tea and sat with us for a bit. I watched the divers as Marcus explained to Gus that he was very low on the police totem pole, that he had a wife and one child, and that he expected the upcoming World Cup of soccer would cause chaos, even in Hamm, far away from the game venues. I supposed that all of this chatter was for my benefit but I was focused on the divers who were now in the water.

One of the dogs had gotten something, but really, it could have been anything: a rat, garbage, anything. The fact that the divers were staying close to the docks still gave me cause to hope they had something definite. Each time a diver came up, however, he would only shake his head. This search was again leading to a dashing of hopes.

One of Marcus's supervisors, Christine Wentzell, came to confirm that the search had indeed led nowhere and they were sending the dogs back and giving up for the day. Marcus followed her from the van. As I watched them walk towards the rest of the rescue team members, I could tell their conversation was growing a little heated. Marcus was doing his best, I thought, in trying to make a point. I do know that he had been struggling with us throughout our ordeal and sensed that he was as committed to finding Tiffany as anyone could be. I thought I should be in this conversation but as I got myself out of the van, Marcus held up a hand to halt me. He walked over to the dog handlers and after a brief discussion returned to the van.

"We are going to take the dogs to another spot."

I soon found out that Marcus was unwilling to allow the dogs to leave until every option was exhausted. As we drove to a bridge to cross the canal, he explained that farther up, about a kilometre, there was a barge turnaround. This was a two-hundred-metre semi-circle cutout in the canal's retaining wall that allowed room for shipping traffic to turn direction without having to go the full length of the system to do so. Through previous days of searching, I was familiar with that particular area.

Marcus explained that the currents of the canal flowed right by this area and that the water in the turnaround was always relatively still, that an object ... or a body ... would likely get stuck here. Then he added, "It has happened before," causing me again to believe that Tiffany was not the first missing person to be lost in these waters. This location would also have some significance in the days to come.

The dogs had already arrived at the cutout, taking their turns going out in the small boats with their handlers and putting noses in the water. Each time, however, the dog would turn and look helplessly at the handler. The water was rough here as well and the winds blowing as hard as the previous location. I think that even if there was a scent present, the conditions were making it too difficult for the dogs. We stayed on and watched in the chill of the February day for only a brief time. We had to concede that to continue in such conditions was pointless.

I didn't know for sure if this day could be considered yet another turning point. Really, nothing had changed; it was just another day that we had failed to find Tiff. I was aware we were now in a bit of a different situation. The authorities were all in agreement that there was really no longer a definite starting point from which to resume a search. Tiffany's body could now be almost anywhere along the entire length of the waterway. (They were also almost unanimously agreeing now that she was in the water somewhere.) I returned to the police station with Gus, Marcus and Christine. The police and search teams were at a loss as to what to do next. Too much time had passed since Tiffany had disappeared. She could be anywhere along the canal system by now and the authorities really had no idea where to start again. Also, commercial shipping traffic on the canal had resumed, making it impossible to have divers in the water for any real length of time.

I stood in the third-floor hallway of the Hamm police department with Angus and Marcus, trying to determine what my next course of action would be. I was feeling completely helpless and as exhausted as I have ever felt. The authorities were admitting they were completely unsure of how to proceed with all the factors we were dealing with now. They believed the only option was to wait – and hope that Tiffany's body would come to the surface somewhere close.

I turned to ask Marcus what he thought I should do. He had experience with similar cases and must have some ideas. I think he was about to suggest I should go back to Nova Scotia to wait for news with my family, that there was nothing else I could do. But as he looked at me and saw my commitment, he stopped. He then told me, as tears started to well in his eyes, that the only thing I could do, at least for the time being, was to continue on my own. "Walk the banks of the canal" was all he could muster.

I do not recall now exactly the mood or tone with which Angus reacted to these words, but I do remember he didn't think that was something I should be doing. I do remember vividly, though, what happened next. Marcus looked at Angus and I believe his exact words were "What would you do if that was your daughter out there?" What had already been a most trying day got even more brutal. Angus turned away and walked down the hall without saying a word. Marcus, after admitting, "I am so sorry," turned away in the other direction. As for me, I could only slump against and then slide down the wall.

We all took a few minutes to gather ourselves and when Angus and Marcus returned, their reddened eyes told me that I was not the only one struggling. Angus admitted he indeed had a thought of one of his precious daughters being lost in those cold, dark, murky waters and it was too much for him to handle. I felt awful for Angus just then. No one should have to endure that image, hypothetical or not. But I also was fully aware (I think it came to me as I was peeling myself off the wall just a minute earlier) that the search for my girl was now entirely on me and, at that moment at least, I was okay with that. I was still as determined as ever to bring Tiffany home. I didn't realize then what lay ahead of me.

The three of us stood together in the hallway for a while longer, not coming up with any brilliant ideas. The look of complete loss and/or frustration on our faces must have been obvious to Christine Wentzell when she came out from the office. I had gotten the impression that Christine was a tough woman, one to tell it as she saw it. She instructed Marcus to call it a day and for Angus and me to do the same. She then turned to Angus and I think I even remember a hint of a smile on her face as she, again in the worst English, told him to take me to have "many beers."

Since I was thoroughly convinced that the Sturms – and in particular Anna, Franz, and Birgit – had to get back to some sort of normality, I had decided to go to a hotel in downtown Hamm at least for a few days. It was also much closer to the canal, police, and club boathouse. Angus was also staying there. Marcus drove us to the hotel as Gus and I decided to rest for a bit and then get something to eat. Angus went to his room to sleep.

I went to my room, opened a beer, and unfolded my map of the city of Hamm and surrounding areas. I tried to determine where I would start my searches in the days ahead. Alexander and I had covered quite a bit of distance in the preceding few days but perhaps Tiffany had come to the surface farther up the canal since then. I was frustrated, not knowing enough about the currents of the canal, how strong they might be from one area to another, or about the effects the locks had on the currents. I also had no idea how commercial traffic might affect things. Marcus was right. The only option I had was to walk, and look – and hope. The hope had changed, though. Initially the hope was that Tiffany would be found alive. Now, it was hope that she would be found.

Angus and I found a small tavern in the downtown area, ordered some food and the first of what really would turn into "many beers." As we ate, we shared stories of our children and their growing years. Angus's two daughters, Annie and Katie, were acquaintances of Tiffany. They had all raced together at a recent national championship regatta in Ontario. We talked of the hopes that we had for our children and what we thought they may end up doing with their lives. We talked of our wives, also lifelong friends with each other, and how they were so good for us, keeping us on the straight and narrow. We sat until the wee hours. The bar staff eventually realized who we were and our purpose for being in Hamm. There are not a lot of English-speaking tourists in Hamm in February. Eventually, Gus and I realized that we were the only patrons left in the place. It had closed and two staff members sat at a table in the back, chatting over a cup of coffee.

We somehow made it back to the hotel to get some sleep. I was up early the next morning and went to walk the canal for a few hours before going back to the hotel to wake Angus. I had decided there was now very little he could do to help at this point, no matter how much he wanted to. Angus also had a family back home and his company to consider. I walked with him to the train station later that morning. It was tough to say goodbye. He had been a comfort since his arrival a couple of days earlier and I was wary about being on my own in the days that lay ahead. But it was obvious that this had become a one-person operation. Gus gave me a hug and wished me well before boarding the train for the airport. I watched the train pull out, then I turned and headed for the canal.

I have been asked a number of times if the Canadian government was of any help during this time. Actually, we had surprisingly little contact or conversation with the Canadian authorities. The day before, however, Margaret Felisiak, a member of the Canadian embassy in Germany, flew in from Berlin to speak with the Hamm authorities as the search was going on, apparently to ensure that it was carried on as long as possible.

Margaret and Willem actually met with an officer, who I believe now was the chief of police or some such. Willem had apparently sensed I did not favour this fellow and thought it best that I sit this meeting out. Angus and I sat on a bench in the hall for this fifteen-minute meeting and as I sat and thought about it, Willem was right. I surely would have said or done something stupid, partly out of frustration and partly because I had a hard time dealing with this man's arrogance.

Margaret later walked with us to the spot where Tiffany was last seen, as well as to where the dogs had searched on that first day. We had lunch, and she headed back to the airport. Again, she was a nice enough lady but what could she really do? She and Willem did manage to convince the authorities to keep the search going with the water police and a helicopter flight over the canal once per day.

After Angus boarded the train that morning, I headed for the canal and spent the remainder of the day walking the banks. This would be the first of a number of truly dark days.

In those days that followed, I stayed close to the same routine, not because I was particularly well-organized, but because I didn't care to think much and went with what seemed right and easiest. I woke at first light in the morning, put a couple of chocolate bars, two or three bottles of water and my binoculars in my knapsack and drove to my parking spot at the turnaround. From there I walked the park side of the canal, opposite the downtown district of Hamm, every day until well after dark. I would eat somewhere easy in the evening, usually a nearby McDonald's; I would then walk back to the hotel to sleep until the following morning when I would start over again.

The citizens of Hamm were, for the most part, sympathetic and supportive and in those first days played a large part in keeping me going. At least two or three times a day, I would be stopped by a person or a couple out walking, who recognized the maple leaf on the back of my coat. They offered their prayers and wishes. I recall one young boy, perhaps fifteen or sixteen years of age. He ran by me on a part of a path that was not very well-travelled. After a few moments, he stopped and came back to me. In his best broken English and with tears rolling down his cheeks, he tried to tell me that all of the people of Hamm were praying for Tiffany and our family and that he also watched for Tiffany during his daily runs. I think I may have given him a hug as I thanked him before continuing on.

On one occasion, sadly, I found that some people were less supportive. A member of the "bad" press that Marcus had warned me about caught up with me even on the rather remote side of the canal. This idiot insisted on standing directly in front of me to take photos as I walked. After pushing by him a few times, my frustration and anger got the best of me and I rolled him down the bank toward the water. This was an act that I was certain would land me in jail, but nothing came of it as it was actually me who decided not to press charges.

The days were long and I became more and more exhausted and my emotional state became more and more fragile. Some days, I had to reverse my steps and backtrack because I was far too goofed up to think and realized I hadn't really been looking as I walked. Other days, I would sit on the canal bank and cry a bit or I would beg Tiffany out loud to find her way home. I was never really aware of how long I would sit. I do know that as time went on, I thought that no parent should ever have to go through this. I was walking the banks of a dirty canal, thousands of miles from my home, alone and looking for the body of my little girl. The truly horrible thing about it was that I think I was hoping to find her.

As the days continued to run together, I completely lost track of which day of the week it was or what the date may have been, and really, it didn't matter a whole lot. I know that every day out, I was sinking more and more. It was like I was walking in quicksand. I sunk deeper and deeper into hopelessness with each step. I was missing Lisa. I was missing Derek and Emma at home. But mostly, I was desperate to find Tiffany, no matter where she was. My lowest point came very late on one of my last days out.

There had been low cloud cover for much of the day and a cold wind blew the canal water into a chop. I walked full into a snow squall during the early to mid afternoon and I found it colder than previous days. By late afternoon the temperature had dipped even lower and darkness was beginning to set in. I had already turned and started back for the car parked, as always, at the turnaround. My shoulders were hunched against the cold and I was at a wider part of the canal watching the opposite shore where bushes and weeds grew out into the water. I thought it a likely place where something or anything might get stuck. I don't recall if I was thinking about anything in particular when I saw her.

There across the canal, perhaps fifty or sixty metres away, was her red shirt, mostly submerged and caught up in the growth. It was her. I had found Tiffany.

I do not recall, as I sit here many months later, if I felt any one thing or perhaps too much to fathom. I knew I had to get to her before it got much darker. It took me perhaps forty-five minutes or so to get to the car, drive back across the bridge to the spot where I thought I had seen her. It was during that forty-five minutes that thoughts began to filter through. Was it really my little girl? Was she really dead? Was I relieved that we had found her and now I could take her home to her mom? We could say goodbye. After a bit of time searching the bushes along the canal, I found our Tiffany again.

It was dark now and my little flashlight was not much help in the thickness of the bushes along the water's edge but I was still certain I had found her. I got a grip on a small tree and fought and stretched my way through the bushes to try to reach my daughter. I was in the canal up to my knees, and the frigid water was numbing me but I still couldn't reach her. I thought about the promise I had made to Lisa and I think that even for me, I had to be the one to bring her home.

I found a branch and waded back in. The weight on the end of the branch made me even more sure that I had found Tiff. More thoughts poured through me as I wrestled with the weight and the bushes. Did I have a blanket in the car to warm her as I had promised Lisa? Where would I take her? The police department? The hospital? Should I call somebody? Finally, I got my now frozen right hand on the object and began to pull.

It felt hard and soft at the same time. Was it supposed to feel that way? I didn't know. I was so scared. It was almost to me now. I got my feet on solid ground and began to pull but it didn't seem right. It was as if she just kept coming. She didn't have arms or legs. I started to panic, thinking that one of the barges on the canal had hit her. But soon it became clear that my efforts were for naught.

I realized that after almost two hours of believing I could take Tiffany home, I was now holding a covering of some sort, a piece of garbage left by one of the many fisherman who used the canal.

I sat in the long grass and stared at nothing. I couldn't determine if I was sad or happy, distraught or relieved. I was just numb and stumbling through a fog. I made it to the car and was able to warm myself for a bit. I sat for what I think was quite a long time wondering if what I had just done was real. I was crying hard and my thoughts were all over the place. Did I only go through

this because I was so desperate and would I have reacted the same way to what I had seen if I was in a better
emotional place? One thing I was sure of was that I was
starting to lose it. Maybe other parents were equipped to
handle this but I was finding out that I was not. I thought
that I would never tell Lisa what I had just done.

Eventually, I made my way back to the boathouse
where I left the car at night. I got out of the car and started to walk in the direction of the hotel but found that I
couldn't remember the way. I was wandering down streets
I didn't recognize. Still wet and getting colder, I started
shivering. I was told later that it was close to midnight local time, when Lisa's sister, Susan, called Tiff's German
cell phone that I was now carrying. I heard her on the
other end but I wasn't really listening. As if it came from
somewhere else, I started sobbing into the phone, "I can't
find her, I can't find Tiff in the water." There I was, sitting on a curb in downtown Hamm, shivering and sobbing with no clue what to do even for the next minute,
never mind the days ahead. The previous days, the days
since we had received that first phone call from Willem,
had taken their toll and I was at my lowest.

When I woke the next morning, I was immediately
aware that I couldn't go back to the canal. I could not
possibly get through another day like the previous one
and absolutely had to do something to get to a better
frame of mind – to recharge my batteries if only for just a
bit. And I was really missing Derek and Emma. I needed
to hug them desperately. But I was torn between that need
and the promise I had made to Lisa. I hoped she would
understand.

By the following day, I was making arrangements to
return home for only a few days. I did have one thing to

do for Tiffany, however, before I left her. I wrote a letter to Tiff trying to explain that I did my best and I was not giving up. I just needed a few days to rest at home and then I would be back. In the meanwhile, I hoped she would keep trying to find her way home to us. And I reminded her that I loved her so very much. I then bought a sturdy picture frame and on the back of the frame, now containing her picture, I attached my letter to Tiffany.

I found a place under the bridge where she had disappeared and secured the frame to the wall, but it was much more difficult to walk away from Tiff that day than I had imagined. I sat by the bridge in the cold and damp of the early morning, again begging her through tears to try as hard as she could to come home to us. As I sat there, I felt so guilty that I was about to abandon Tiffany, to leave her on her own. I knew I would be back within a few days, a week at the most, but I still couldn't find the courage to drag myself up and start for home until hours later.

One of the many people who had been so supportive throughout our travel back and forth to Germany was my friend and concierge with Air Canada in Halifax. Carol Baldwin, a good friend for a number of years beforehand, not only helped me to arrange flights and connections home but also suggested that I not fly alone in my emotional stupor. I passed it off, thinking that there was no way I was going to ask a family member to fly to Germany just to turn around and fly right home again. I was sure I would make it on my own.

The plan ran into some complications when my flight from Dortmund to my connecting flight in Frankfurt was delayed. I was cutting it close as it was. Because the Frankfurt airport is absolutely massive, I was certain I could not get from Arrivals to Departures in time to make my connection. I was able to discover that the next flight out from Frankfurt didn't leave until the following day. My prospects for the next twenty-four hours did not appear too bright.

Upon landing, however, I learned that Carol had things completely under control. The flight attendants hurried me off the plane in Frankfurt where, just inside the gate, I found Carol waiting, complete with airport cart and driver. I remember being absolutely overwhelmed that she would fly some nine hours from Halifax to Germany (via Montreal or Toronto) only to fly back an hour later. That kind of compassion is rare.

She also chose cart drivers wisely. The young lady at the wheel was, I want to say reckless, but I'll go with wickedly efficient. It took no more than ten minutes to get to our connection and that included a bit of a hassle at Security. The long haul and fatigue did take a toll on Carol. She struggled a bit to start the return flight but quickly righted herself and was able to make the flight more than bearable. Too much time to think would have been a bad thing. I hope Carol really understands just how much that sacrifice is still appreciated.

Tiffany with her favourite horse, Scottish Dancer.

Tiff and Dad finishing the Natal Day two-miler, 1992.

My favourite picture of Tiffany, dancing with sister Emma at cousin Jody's wedding.

Tiff, Derek and Emma in Europe, 2002.

In Teneriefe, 2005.

Lisa and me with Tiff's cross on the bank of the Datteln-Hamm canal in August 2006.

Christmas 2005 during Tiff's last time home.

TIFFANY FINDS HER WAY HOME

Lisa and I would often return home to find Tiffany planted squarely in front of the television with a large brick of chedder melted over a large bag of nachos and accompanied by a new bottle of salsa. Telephone and cellular phone were never far away.

I have never been a believer in anything spiritual and I don't remember now exactly how the idea of seeking help from a medium or spiritualist came to me. I will allow for the likelihood that Carol put it into my head in our conversation during our flight home, but when I got off the plane in Halifax, one of the first things I said to Lisa was "We are going to see a psychic." Again, I was never a believer but I was desperate and knew I had nothing to lose. I also knew I needed some idea where to start looking once I returned to Hamm a few days later.

Another of my good friends, Elaine Keene, was a believer and had spoken about a few people in the "spirit business." Elaine had the names of a few people who claimed to have a special ability to locate and/or communicate with the dead.

After a few telephone calls, we had an appointment the next day with a local lady named Evelyn Hare. Evelyn had a calming voice on the phone and spoke matter-of-factly about what she did. She informed me she had helped with missing persons cases in the past, sometimes with success. Lisa and I were to meet her at her home the following evening.

Lisa and I found Evelyn's small, well-kept home after a twenty-minute drive. She welcomed us in and to her credit, she did not mince words. Before we even sat down, she informed Lisa and me that Tiffany was "no longer among the living." We were taken aback a bit by her bluntness but it was the possibility that we considered most likely.

The three of us sat at Evelyn's kitchen table and she asked us a number of questions about Tiffany and how she came to be missing. As she was speaking, Evelyn would make comments about Tiffany, comments about traits that would only be known to those who had met Tiffany. Tiffany could be and was a loyal good friend to people who she called true friends. She sometimes seemed older than she was and Lisa and Tiffany were soul mates. Of course, Lisa and Tiffany were close but unless you had ever been around the two, you would never understand just how connected they were. Evelyn even commented on how Tiffany was smaller in stature than Lisa.

She explained how she arrived at the conclusions she did by using her charts, which were astrology based. Between our phone conversation and our meeting, Evelyn had made what she called a chart on Tiffany. She told us that in using Tiffany's birth chart, the feeling of death could not be stronger. She was also as sure as we were that Tiff had not run away; she was receiving too much positive energy (positive energy is a common theme in this regard). Tiff's charts even indicated that she would be far from home when she died. So far, everything Evelyn said to this point made sense or was at least not far off.

She then began to tell Lisa and me about Tiffany's existence here on earth, not just in this lifetime but in past lifetimes as well. Evelyn told us this was Tiffany's sixth lifetime on earth and that in five of her previous lives on earth, Tiff had been a male. She told us, among other things, that Tiffany had been a member of royalty or, at the very least, nobility and had also served in an army. She told us Tiff had always been sports-minded and she had always been around horses in her previous lifetimes. Lisa and I later wondered why or how Evelyn thought it necessary to mention Tiff's fondness for horses. She also told us Lisa had been with Tiffany in all of her previous lifetimes and they would be together in their lifetimes ahead, six or so.

Evelyn was very adamant that everyone has a life plan that cannot be changed, a kind of manifest destiny. There was nothing that could have been done to prevent Tiffany's death; it was simply "her time." Again, Evelyn spoke so matter-of-factly that she made it very easy to believe what she was telling us.

But we still did not have the answers to our questions that most needed answering. Where was Tiffany now? How long would it be before we would be able to bring her home?

I completely understand that there are many people who simply do not buy into any ideas about life after death, never mind people actually "communicating with" or "seeing" what spirits might see. All or most of what Evelyn said to us next would prove to have some merit.

She told us she had put herself in Tiffany's mind or body and allowed herself to go through Tiff's accident. Evelyn knew that the accident was exactly that – an accident. She felt that something had hit Tiff's boat, perhaps another boat or wash. She knew that Tiff was very close to the canal bank, within feet. She told us the accident happened very quickly and that Tiffany was unconscious almost immediately. She told us of her vision of Tiffany sliding straight down a flat wall in dirty or silt-filled water and that there would be a hole or something round nearby, something with a grate or lines over it, perhaps a water feed or intake.

There is no way that Evelyn could have possibly known, but under the bridge where Tiffany had disappeared, there is indeed a concrete retaining wall that extends vertically down to the canal floor and there is a grated water feed for street runoff on that wall. The water is particularly dark at this location due to that runoff. Again, and because there was no way that Evelyn could know of these things, I wondered how much there could actually be to this psychic phenomenon.

Before we left, Evelyn held a sweater, one of Tiff's favourites, and confessed to feeling so much energy in her arms and shoulders. From this she felt that Tiffany was trying very hard to reach her mother and that she was here with us. This revelation left Lisa and me even more desperate to bring her home and we pressed Evelyn. Did she have any idea at all when the authorities in Hamm might have any success or any idea as to where I might start my search when I travelled back to Hamm?

Of course, Evelyn could not tell us anything for certain but encouraged Lisa and me to light two green candles when we got home and put them in the window (something we have done every night since, and still do today). She thought that by doing this, we may get a sign from Tiffany. This sign might be so subtle that it may not be recognized, perhaps a bird outside the window or her favourite song on the radio. Evelyn thought we would know something of Tiffany's fate near the end of the month, some three weeks away.

Lisa and I spoke a little on the way home and concluded that in some instances, Evelyn could have gained information from the media and some would have been easy enough to make up. Nevertheless, she did say some things that were mind-bending enough for me to know that I was in fact going to light the two green candles that evening and put them in the window. I had nothing to lose. What transpired over the next eight hours or so has left me forever a believer that there is contact with the afterlife.

As a side note, during our time sitting at Evelyn's kitchen table she mentioned to us, more as an idle or passing comment than anything else, that over the next three years, children and young adults would become victims and/or die of many different causes. In the months since we have lost a number of teenagers and young adults as a result of everything from traffic accidents, murder, and even something as simple as a seizure. In my home province of Nova Scotia, one need only do a bit of research to know that Evelyn was extraordinarily accurate.

And so I did light my candles, green, the colour of Tiffany's birthstone, and I put them in the front window. Again, I had nothing to lose and in our desperation would try anything. I sat quietly in Tiff's room for a while before going to bed.

I had decided I would call the authorities in Hamm every morning as their day was beginning. I wanted to be sure that they would not forget about our daughter and to keep searching for her. So I set my bedside alarm for 2:30 a.m. (7:30 a.m. in Hamm), turned off the light and tried to sleep. What sleep I was able to get over the next three hours was broken by restlessness and my mind was consumed with the thoughts of all that had happened to our family over the last two-plus weeks. And of course, I thought of Tiffany. Where was she? I found myself thinking, hoping, praying, that perhaps she was still alive. The authorities in Germany, Evelyn, the media, even Lisa and I ... we could be wrong. It had been many days and since we hadn't found her, or "seen" her, perhaps she was alive, somewhere.

Rising with the alarm at 2:30 a.m. on Wednesday March 8, 2006, was not difficult as my sleep was somewhat hindered anyway. I sat on the side of the bed for a moment, dreading the calls I was about to make for fear of being told what we actually needed to hear. I put on some sweat clothes to go downstairs. I first felt my way to the other side of the bed to cover Lisa and give her a kiss on the cheek before leaving the room. The stairs and the kitchen were dark, save for a small light over the kitchen counter as I passed through on my way to the family room.

As I entered the family room I turned to my left to switch on one of two lamps in the room and then turned to walk to the phone only ten feet away. As I turned, I froze where I was. Standing in front of me, just three feet in front of me, was Tiffany. Wearing one of her favourite red sweatshirts, as solid as you or me, and with an almost apologetic look was our little girl. There was no ghostly appearance, no transparency. Tiff was as real as life and standing with me in our family room.

The experience lasted for perhaps five or six seconds but in those seconds, I was flooded with so many different emotions. I admit I felt fear but I think it was because I just didn't know what this meant. That fear was followed by disbelief, then relief and then hope. Tiffany stood in front of me long enough to cause me to think that she was real and that she was really there. But as I fell half a step back against the doorjamb, I blinked my eyes and when I opened them again, Tiffany was gone. I so wish now that I hadn't blinked. How long would Tiffany have stayed with me? Would she have spoken to me? I am thankful now that I did have this experience. To us, it meant that Tiffany was truly able to find her way home to us, but I do still wonder.

I know that I sat on the love seat next to the telephone and shook, still amazed by what had happened only moments before. Evelyn was, to state the very least, right on with the green candles. If Tiff standing in front of me for more than five seconds could not be taken as a sign, well, certainly nothing could. I do not even know now how long I sat before finally finding my way to the kitchen to make some tea to try to calm down.

I thought perhaps I would wake Lisa and tell her that Tiffany had found her way home but really, how would she accept such a thing? She may think Tiff's being here to be a confirmation of her death or, on the other hand, a sign that she was still alive somewhere. Or maybe she would think I was flipping out and since I was trying to be the wing nut that held us together, the thought of waking Lisa quickly left my head.

I did eventually try to make my calls to Hamm. I tried to get through to the police, the water police and the fire department without much success. In some instances, dialing all of the correct numbers was the issue, but mostly, language was the main stumbling block. The officers I spoke to undoubtedly recognized my name but were unable to converse in English or find anyone else who might be able to. This left me frustrated, exhausted again, and still very unsure of myself due to Tiff's earlier visit.

My last call was to Kattia, hoping perhaps she would be up to making some calls for me but also because I knew she had been struggling as well. Maybe hearing my voice could bring her some comfort. It was now approaching 4:30 a.m. Kattia told me she and Willem were dealing with all things concerned with the search, the German media, and their own grief. She assured me she would try to find out if there were any new developments and try to call me back later in the day. We encouraged each other to take care of ourselves before saying goodbye and then I hung up the phone.

I was tired but didn't know if sleep was going to happen. Perhaps I would just go up and lie with Lisa for a bit before getting up. It had only been a minute or so, I think, since I had hung up the phone and I was about to switch off the lamp beside the door when the phone rang again.

It immediately came into my head that Tiff would be with me again when I turned around but that didn't happen. I remember thinking that no good news was going to come from a telephone call at 4:30 a.m, so I was reluctant to pick up the phone. It could be the press again, or perhaps the authorities in Hamm had found an English-speaking someone to catch me up on developments.

I was relieved to hear Kattia's voice again. It had been less than two minutes – she must have forgotten something. Instead, her voice was weak and halting.

"They have found Tiffany in the water" was all she could manage.

The next voice I heard was Marcus's. He and Johan Bosch must have been in the Sturms' driveway and walking to the door just as Kattia and I were saying goodbye only moments before. From his tone and broken speech, I was certain this was a conversation Marcus did not want to have. He told me a harbour worker had found Tiffany's body early that morning as he was reporting for work. Truly, I didn't know what to ask or what was important at that point. He told me Tiffany had been found at the turnaround shortly after 7:00 a.m. and that the fire service had gotten her out of the water just past 7:30.

I dreaded asking the only question that I really needed an answer to but I had to know: "What condition was her body in? Have you seen her?"

His voice was low and his tone apologetic as he told me he had seen Tiffany before driving to the Sturms. "Her body is in very good condition and she looks very good" but he had then halted, probably realizing how that sounded. I knew it because I was thinking it too. But really, how else could he have presented such a fact? Under the circumstances, this was the good in the worst news.

I told Marcus I just couldn't think, but I was sure I would have more questions for him after I had some time to absorb what he had just told me and I would call him back later on in the day.

Time stood still, at least in the few minutes after hanging up the phone, too many thoughts going through my mind. What we knew in our hearts all along was now a fact. Our very faintest of hopes that Tiffany may still be alive somewhere out there were now extinguished. I did realize even now, moments after Marcus's confirmation, that I was thankful. Lisa and I had talked about the possibility that we may never get Tiffany back, ever. But now we could bring her home. We could say goodbye to our girl and let others do the same.

I, of course, had to break the news to Lisa but had no clue as to what might be a best way to do it. Should I tell her now or wait till she woke? Was this the relief we had been waiting for or was the finality too much to bear? Or was it just the beginning of our nightmare of knowing for absolute certain now that we would have to live our lives without Tiffany?

Lisa and I had to get to Hamm to be with Tiff and to bring her home. I had to arrange a flight. Lisa would want to see Tiffany when she got there. I, again, was completely panicked at the thought of Lisa's last vision or memory of Tiffany being less than perfect. I knew even then that I wanted to protect Lisa from that. All of these thoughts went through my mind and I didn't know what to do first but really, there was only one thing. I climbed the stairs to wake Lisa.

Nothing in this world can possibly prepare you for breaking this kind of news to the person you truly love. As I sat on our bed watching Lisa in her restless sleep, I dreaded the next moments. I rubbed Lisa's shoulder until she stirred and opened her eyes and was able to find my face.

"I want you to sit up for me." The tears in my eyes I'm sure were a giveaway but I had to get the words out anyway. "They have found Tiffany."

Those words were simply a confirmation for Lisa and I did not have to tell her how it had turned out. Her baby was dead and Lisa now knew that the last one percent of hope was gone and that it was final. All I could do was hold her. Her pain over the last number of days had been so intense. Nothing I could say to my wife at that moment was going to make things better for her.

"I can't live without her." A pause and then again, "I can't live without her."

I didn't have a response to her statement right away but then held each of her shoulders and said with all the strength I could muster, "Yes you can, and you will. You will because you have always been the most incredible mother and now you have two children who are going to need you." But as I held Lisa, I silently wondered how I would do without Tiff in my life.

I do recall at least some of what I did over the next couple of hours. I first called Susan to tell her and to ask if she would call the others in the family. Her husband, Doug, answered the phone. I think my first words were that they had found Tiffany. Susan's reaction in the background – "Oh, thank God" – caused me at first to believe she thought I meant they had found Tiffany alive. I would guess now that I then explained rather quickly that they had found Tiffany in the water and she was not alive. I asked Susan if she would call everyone in the family while I tried to arrange a flight to Germany.

I recalled Lisa, or someone, telling me that Lisa's boss might be able to help with flights to Europe if we needed it, but I knew after just a few moments of speaking with him on the phone that he was too upset, at least at that time. So I called and woke my good friend, Brad Murray, at Air Canada. After explaining to him the circumstances under which Lisa and I had to get to Germany, he immediately set out to do all that he could to arrange flights. I believe it was getting close to 6:30 a.m. when members of the family began to arrive.

I had wakened Derek and Emma to tell them Tiffany had died and that Lisa and I were going to go to Germany to bring her home. I have always worried about D and Em and how they were really coping. Emma for the most part tells us everything she is thinking, but she had been missing Tiffany so much. She was also the one in our family who seemed to hold onto the most hope that Tiff would come home again and that they would share sister times and shopping expeditions and going for donuts together. Emma hurt so badly, but we knew she was hurting and could deal with that.

It was Derek who had me so worried. We were told he had spent too much time on his own since the news of Tiffany's disappearance. D was never one to talk about how he is feeling. He kept most things inside and it was so on the morning of March 8th. He stayed by himself in the basement rec room and didn't come up or say much. Lisa's sisters kept going downstairs to try to get him to come upstairs to be with the rest of the family but he insisted on being alone. I recall telling him to do what he was comfortable doing but if he had any questions or wanted to talk, to find me and I would try to help. I went to him hourly just to check with him but for the most part left him in his comfort zone.

It was close to 7:00 a.m. and the house was now filled with family. The morning news was broadcasting reports of Tiffany being found in Germany but I don't believe any of us could watch. We knew what we needed to know. A family friend walked by on her way to work and I could only watch as she stared at our house and cried. Lisa's sisters and her niece made calls to inquire about insurance coverages and I did my best to help with these needs. Friends called often over the course of the day to offer their support and help, including money for travel if we needed it. The house was very busy in those first few hours.

Emma and I went for a number of walks together. I let Emma talk and I did my best to answer the questions she had. I was aware it just wasn't really sinking in for Em and was concerned that it would happen during the days ahead when Lisa and I would be in Hamm.

For Lisa's part, she stayed on the couch, a blanket over her, and was quiet for the day. She was able to sleep a bit, I think, and I would sit with her for stretches but really, she spent the day with her own grief, her mind and thoughts seemingly oblivious to everyone else.

It was late in the day, after flights had been confirmed, insurance issues dealt with, the house still filled with family but quieter when I went upstairs to Tiff's room, closed the door, cried and remembered my daughter. I remembered more from her growing years of paddling, Christmas times, zoo visits, drives to dance class. I remembered our more recent times together. Our trip to Germany and the Czech Republic just months earlier. Sharing beers at the Hofbrauhaus in Munich, touring Rothenburg, walking through Prague to watch the old town come to life at night. There are rows of benches directly across from the Tyne church in the Prague town square. Tiff and I sat for hours during one of our evenings there. We watched the tourists window shop. We watched the locals and the homeless drink beer and wine from their soda bottles. But mostly, we just talked.

We talked of Tiffany's expectations for the coming year: of her fears of not being able to communicate enough to get by, of perhaps not being able to handle her new duties and of her fear of being homesick. By this, I knew she meant that she was going to miss her mom. Lisa was, and I'm sure still is, everything to Tiff. The two of them will always have a bond envied by others. I reminded Tiffany then that both her mom and I were so proud of her for having the courage to leave home for such a long period. That at first, things would seem so new to her and perhaps difficult, but that these things would pass.

I knew this was a big step for a girl like Tiff. She was shy and her family was her entire life. I remembered laughing and teasing her during our short tour. I remembered how charming it was that Tiff was too shy to order at McDonald's but was about to spend a year entrenched in this culture. "You won't last a week," I would tease her. And I remembered how she came back at Christmas time a confident young woman, speaking constantly about how much she had come to enjoy her time away, about the new friends she had met and about how much she was learning about life and herself.

Mostly, however, I thought of how much I was going to miss Tiffany. We had truly grown closer over recent years, sharing more. I was so very proud of her and was so excited by the opportunities her new-found confidence would bring. There was so much that Lisa and I were looking forward to in the coming years: boyfriends, university, careers, weddings and, hopefully some day, grandchildren. We were so happy with our family and were starting to look forward to growing old together and enjoying our relationships with all of our children. That is now gone. Lisa and I now had to find a way to get through the overwhelming grief that was just starting and if we got through that, a way to cope for all the years to follow.

Returning to Hamm

Tiff was at her most charming when listening to others relate any unbelievable story. She had a way of crinkling her nose up with a look of complete incredulity that always made us melt.

I do not recall much of the return trip to Germany. There was really nothing I could say to Lisa during our travel. We left late in the evening and our itinerary included a stopover in St. John's, Newfoundland. The snow was falling quite heavily in St. John's, risking our takeoff. I know both Lisa and I spoke little and tried to get some rest. We might have been successful had it not been for a couple of Finnish fellows who had boarded the plane in a drunken stupor and were both loud and particularly obnoxious. It was not until the plane had been de-iced a third time and we were an hour or so into our flight that the cabin was finally quiet enough to rest a bit.

There was that one thought that had been troubling me almost since we had received the news of Tiffany being found and for some time before. I knew Lisa and I knew she would want to see Tiffany when we arrived in Hamm. This worried me only because I did not want Lisa's last memory of Tiffany to be anything less than it should have been. The last time Lisa saw her, Tiffany was happy and had her amazing "Tiff smile" working. It was at the Halifax airport on the day she left us after her Christmas visit to return to Germany. She was still smiling, waving to us as she passed through the security gate.

This time, however, the reality was it would be only Tiffany's physical body that we would see. There would be no smile, no warm hugs, no "I've missed you." I had to find a way to convince Lisa that seeing Tiffany may be just too difficult, if not now then in the weeks, months and years to come. The reality was our Tiffany had spent seventeen days in the frigid waters of the Datteln-Hamm canal. I supposed it to be an understandable assumption that she would not look like our Tiffany. But really, I had no idea what to expect. I just knew it couldn't possibly be what we wanted to remember and I had to find a way to spare Lisa.

When I did broach the subject with Lisa, she fought me as I knew she would. I tried to hold steadfast, hoping she might decide that it might be too much after all. Eventually, and I believe now that she was simply too mentally exhausted to fight me on the issue any longer, Lisa agreed to trust me with the decision. She agreed that when we arrived at the undertaker's in Hamm, I would go in to see Tiffany first and if then I thought Tiffany's appearance was something that Lisa could deal with, then she would go in to say goodbye. I truly did not know if this was something I would be able to deal with, but I was very sure that it was the lesser of the two evils.

After Tiffany was found in Hamm, a number of other things occurred to me. Some may only be coincidence but still, I wonder. I thought back to the phone call from Kattia and Marcus on that awful morning when Tiffany was found but more particularly to the timing of Tiff's being found. Marcus told me that Tiffany was seen in the water just after 7:00 a.m. in Germany and that they were able to get to her and bring her out of the water just after 7:30. When it was 7:30 in Hamm, it was only 2:30 a.m. in Dartmouth. This meant that at almost exactly the same minute that Tiffany was being taken from the water in Hamm, she was with me in our family room.

Marcus also told me that Tiffany was found at the west side of the barge turnaround at the canal. This is approximately two kilometres from where she went missing. This spot is no more than fifty feet or so from where I parked the car every morning during my days of searching. If Tiffany was stuck at that place in the turnaround for any length of time at all, she was likely no more than a stone's throw from me every morning during my search, but I had no way of knowing. Lastly, Evelyn Hare had told us less than ten hours before Tiffany was found that she saw Tiffany being in a place where there might be a circle or round area and there were lines or a grill on the wall. Coincidence or no, the barge turnaround is a semi-circle, its retaining wall being a heavy, corrugated, steel wall with straight, perpendicular, reinforcing ridges every twelve inches or so. I will let readers draw their own conclusions from this.

Beyond the two Finnish yahoos, our flight was uneventful. As with every other flight during our entire ordeal, we were met as we left the plane at London's Heathrow airport by an Air Canada concierge. Again, the

staff of Air Canada were incredibly helpful and supportive at every stop along the way. We were escorted via bus,
cart, escalator, and various other means of transport to the
Departures area to wait for our flight to Düsseldorf.

I watched other travellers during our various rides.
Some were rushing to make connecting flights, some pa-
tiently waited while plugged into one type of electronic
device or another, and others looked particularly helpless, lost for any direction in this massive complex. The
same thought stayed with me as I watched those around
us. Their lives, while perhaps panicked for the moment,
would be normal again at some point. Routines would
return to normal, careers would move forward, families would reunite, their lives would continue along their
paths and time would move on.

For Lisa and me, time was standing still. We were absolutely stuck in our moment. We had no thought of to-
morrow, or next week, or any time in the future. There
was nobody around us who could know where we were.
Life went on. Everyone's life was moving forward – everyone's life but ours. I recall a young lady sat across from
us on the bus between terminals, her arm around her
young son. I tried a weak smile and nodded hello. She
smiled and nodded back having no clue as to what Lisa
and I were coping with. Really, how can anyone know?

It caused me to wonder how many people I have
passed by, not knowing or caring about anything but what
was in front of me. Now, when I people watch, I often
wonder what their lives have left them with. I find this
particularly so with older folks. As I see people on the
street, some have worn or weathered faces with hunched
bodies and conversely, there are others who seem to have
had a very easy life or have aged well. I often wonder if

there is a correlation. Is it as simple as those looking haggard having a rougher life than others? Are the diva-looking older ladies simply fortunate enough to have lived without any serious heartache? I guess in the long run, it doesn't benefit me one way or the other to know these things. People watching is just an interesting way to pass time.

Lisa and I were tired when we finally arrived at the Sturms' home. I couldn't say that it was more difficult to be there now. I suppose it was more like a *déjà vu*.

I recall being met at the door by young Franz. His first question to Lisa was "Are you sad that Tiffany has died?"

"Yes I am," Lisa replied. "Are you sad too?"

Franz was very matter-of-fact with his response. "Yes, I am sad … but not so sad as you." How does the saying go? Kids say the darnedest things.

It is the small down moments such as that day, when there was really nothing for Lisa and me to do except wait, that I have difficulty remembering. I don't remember now how Lisa and I spent the majority of that morning and early afternoon, how we passed those few hours before going to see our daughter. It's my best guess that we just sat at the kitchen table in a daze, our fog created by fatigue, perhaps still a bit of disbelief, and an incredible amount of grief. It was late in the afternoon when Kattia, Lisa and I left the house for the twenty-minute drive to the funeral home. The day was already dark with cloud and dampness. It almost seemed fitting.

We were met at the door by Herr Bulmer, the owner of the funeral home. I wouldn't say now that this man was cold. I would say that he was all business. He was cordial but beyond that, there was very little to indicate that he had ever contemplated a career past this one. The four of us sat at a small table in a side office and the owner did his best to explain, mostly to Kattia in German, exactly what they had done for Tiffany. We were warned that Tiffany had lost her hair, a circumstance of being so long in the water. We were told there had been a start to decomposition, although it was minimal, again the cold water playing a factor. Any injuries that Tiffany sustained, most of them minor and postmortem, were on her legs, arms, and torso so they would not be visible to us when we saw her. Kattia had brought a scarf to be put on Tiffany's scalp, just to make her look a bit more presentable. Then Herr Bulmer took a few moments to leave the room to place the scarf.

I took that time to tell Kattia, and remind Lisa, of the plan Lisa and I had agreed to. I was still extremely wary of Lisa seeing Tiffy if it might be too much. When Herr Bulmer returned to ask if we were ready to go in, I quickly stood to say I would go in to see Tiffany first. I do not know what he thought. I think my eagerness surprised him a bit. He could not have known that I was in protection mode.

As I was leaving the room, all I could do was lay my hand on Lisa's shoulder, but I was so unsure of so many things. I didn't want to leave Lisa alone. I did not know how I would tell Lisa if I thought seeing Tiffany might be too difficult. And I truly did not know what to expect in the next moments. The only thing I did know for sure was that this was something I had to do. I was led down the wide hallway to a large room. Off that room were a number of smaller rooms. We stood outside one of them.

Herr Bulmer unlatched the door, said something to me in German and turned away. I know that I did not go into the room right away. I stood outside the door and I believe that I was shaking. I was even thinking in the back of my mind that it may not even be Tiffany on the other side of the door. I was finding it hard to catch my breath, a condition that would stay with me for many more months whenever I would think of Tiffany. Finally, I put my hand on the doorknob, pushed the door open and stepped inside.

Tiffany lay there and, although it seems odd now, I believe that my first thought was that she looked so tiny. I believe I thought this before I even really identified this young girl as being Tiffany. It wasn't that I couldn't tell you that it was Tiffany – she really did look so much better than I had expected. Again, I don't know what my expectation was. She looked like our Tiffany, but I think the situation still just didn't seem real.

Then the true value of what was in front of me hit me. This was my little girl. I stood at the door almost not wanting to disturb her. I lost my breath again and although tears started almost immediately, I remained quiet. I finally walked to Tiffany and literally fell to my knees beside the low bed that she lay upon. She looked so tiny and so peaceful, but it was our Tiffy. I remember placing my hands on hers and gently touching her face.

I don't know that I took a breath the entire time I was alone with Tiff or how long I was in that small room with her. I'd like to say I was brave and that I dealt with having to say goodbye to Tiffany's physical presence so well but that would be a lie. I have never struggled so badly with my emotions. I apologized to her over and over again but for nothing in particular. And I thanked her for allowing me to be a part of her life. I reminded her that I was so proud of the young lady she had become. But mostly, I just kept telling my little girl that I loved her so much and that I always would.

It took what seemed like a long time to gather the strength to stand and leave the room, even though I was going to bring Lisa back to her in just minutes. For all logical thinking, it was an easy decision to tell Lisa that she should see Tiffany to say goodbye. Tiffany looked so peaceful, as if she truly were at rest. I returned to the office and walked immediately to Lisa. I knelt in front of her and took her hands.

"It is our Tiffany. I think you should come in to see her. You should go and say goodbye."

I guess it was apparent to the others in the office that I had had a difficult time. The swollen, red eyes were a giveaway. I returned to Tiffany with Lisa. It almost destroyed me to see Lisa in this much pain. I do not regret, for even a moment, Lisa's seeing Tiffany on that evening but it is still the most difficult thing I have ever or will ever go through. Lisa just kept touching her and sobbing, "My girl, my baby girl" over and over again. I didn't speak much. I just stayed beside Lisa, trying even in this worst of circumstances to know if Lisa might be going into shock. I wanted to and was really trying so very hard to stay strong for Lisa. I lost. We stayed with Tiffany, well, until we couldn't stay any longer. It was obviously so difficult to leave our daughter there.

It was hard being back out in the hallway when we really still wanted to be with Tiffany. Lisa and I had a difficult time leaving her even now. Kattia hugged each of us. As she hugged me, with tears in her eyes she said to me, "You are so brave." I didn't feel particularly brave at that moment. I don't think I really felt much of anything. I was an absolute mess. I believe there may have been some discussion as to insurance and the travel arrangements that had to be made to get Tiffany home. I think I just nodded my head a lot and held Lisa close.

I am even more grateful to Kattia as I think back now. She dealt with it all so well. The language barrier of course was an obstacle that she was well aware Lisa and I needed help with, but she really left nothing to chance even though she was struggling mightily as well.

We were eventually able to leave the undertaker's for the drive back to the Sturms' home. It was dark now and the drive seemed long, or perhaps I only remember it that way. I don't recall much of the remainder of that evening and I'm sure if I were to ask my wife, she would remember just as little. I assume we just sat at the kitchen table again and talked about Tiff, maybe a little about the things that we still had to do.

There were a number of issues that kept us from returning to Canada right away. We had to wait until the undertaker was able to release Tiffany to us and this all depended on a number of things. Foremost, of course, was the completion of the police investigation, including autopsy results. It seemed straightforward to Lisa and me based on the facts we had. Apparently, the Hamm police were going to make certain that alcohol or drugs were not a factor. As I say, it was straightforward to us.

There was also the issue of travel. The one thing I knew for certain was that I was not returning home without my little girl this time. So I spent quite a bit of time on the phone with Air Canada, doing all we could to ensure that Tiffany would be on the same flights we were. Carol Baldwin, again, came to our rescue. She spent much time, and was extraordinarily diligent, in being certain that things would work out as we needed them to.

There was some initial confusion, due mostly to the uncertainty of release dates. There was also the issue of exactly which city we would re-enter Canada through. The last thing we needed or wanted was a hassle at Customs. Most of that work should and would have been taken care of by the authorities from each country but one never knows.

Lisa and I were not aware (or perhaps just too distracted) to know that Kattia was putting a service together for Tiffany. I suppose if we had thought about it, we would have realized that Tiffany had made quite a few friends during her eight months in Hamm. And the executive and membership at Tiff's kayak club were also struggling with the events of the past weeks. And of course, Willem, Kattia, and the children were trying to cope as well. Tiffany had been a part of their family and a major part of the children's lives for the past eight months. The ordeal had left them reeling as well. Doing something that would allow them a time to say goodbye to Tiffany was important. So the delay with arrangements enabled just that opportunity.

Lisa and I both knew we had to go to the canal to see exactly where Tiffany had been found. We both had a need to know the exact spot, right down to the square foot. Lisa and I took it upon ourselves to drive into town to the police station the next morning. Our plan was to find Marcus or perhaps Johan or Christine. Surely, they could make time to take us to the site. The morning was bright and not terribly cold when we found a parking spot just outside the building. I had by now become quite familiar with the building and we walked directly to the third floor.

It was Marcus who found us first as we were walking

by an office door. It was an emotional reunion. I believe the last time I had seen Marcus was at that very same spot in the hallway as he was advising me to "walk the banks."

I don't know that Lisa and I were totally unexpected by any of the officers. The detectives knew us well by this point and I'm sure they knew we would want all the information they could give us. Marcus and Christine did not hesitate to take us to the canal and we were on our way soon after. The turnaround is on the opposite side of the canal from the downtown area and the police station. We had to get to a bridge as well as fight the unusually busy morning traffic. As a result, the drive was a long one. Marcus seemed to take this personally and his driving showed it.

We drove the dirt road on the opposite side of the canal toward the barge turnaround, beside a path I had come to know all too well. I couldn't help but feel nauseous as Marcus rolled the car to a stop at almost exactly the same spot I had parked the Smart car almost every day during my search. The four of us got out of the car together and Marcus pointed to the spot where Tiffany was taken out of the water. The two officers then turned away and left Lisa and me alone to sit for a while.

It was some closure, I think. We still hurt so incredibly but there was no more uncertainty, no more panic. It was what it was and we now knew what was in front of us. I don't believe it made things easier for us, perhaps just a little more calming. We sat for a while, not speaking. We just sat together and thought, and remembered.

I don't know how long we sat but Marcus and Christine allowed us all the time we wanted. We eventually rose and walked back to the car, knowing we would be back here in the next few days and then for years afterward.

The drive back to the station seemed longer and I began to feel sick again on the way, although it wasn't a physical sickness – probably more of an "I can't cope" thing. Marcus was also having a difficult time holding it together. I looked up to see his eyes in the rear-view mirror and they were red and swollen. I watched as Christine reached over and put her hand on his shoulder. She said something to him, a hushed and calming tone in German. Marcus just nodded his head. I again thought to myself that he really wasn't suited to this type of work.

I was relieved to step out of the car back at the station. We spoke a little more and shook hands with the officers. As Lisa and I left the station, we really had no direction. There was nothing for us to do. We had to wait for what might be days before we were able to leave for home. The odd concern about travel or insurance had to be addressed but it was more just waiting for release and other documents to be completed. For the most part, all we had to do was exist for the next couple of days.

During the days, Lisa and I would go into the city and walk by the canal or we would walk through the downtown stores or the one large mall. Lisa went into every store we could find looking for a special type of small glass heart. When Tiffany was home at Christmas just ten weeks before, she had told us she had found these small glass hearts in Hamm and that she wanted to bring one home for everyone in the family for Christmas but she couldn't afford it. Lisa took it upon herself to complete this task for Tiffany. Now, everyone in our extended family has one of Tiffy's glass hearts.

While in one store in particular, as we were in the process of emptying the shelves of their glass heart inventory, a lady behind the counter recognized us. We did have maple leafs on the back of our coats but I got the feeling that Tiffany had also been in the store at one time. She spoke absolutely no English so we had no real way of finding out. This nice lady insisted upon giving us gifts before we left the store. This was an example of the way we were received throughout the city. Whether it was in English or German, people would come to us on the street and offer us their best wishes. The people in the city were truly amazing in their support.

Another of the things Tiffany had brought home during Christmas was a small figurine of a beach chair. Tiff had explained that the life-sized versions of these chairs were padded, covered, wicker love seats that she had seen on the northern German island of Juist. She told us she never could figure out the German translation for these seats, so she called them "human baskets." She loved them and told us at Christmas that she was going to try to figure a way to get one home to Dartmouth. Lisa and I happened to be passing through a small deserted mall during one of our morning outings when we saw these chairs that Tiff had been so excited about. There were a number of types and styles and it became immediately obvious that we would have to get one of these beach chairs home. We took the company name home with us and in May, just four months after Tiffany's death, we took delivery of Tiff's "human basket." It sits on our front porch now, inviting visitors to our home to share a few moments with Tiffy if they like.

Lisa and I were aware, obviously, that we were going to take Tiffany home to say goodbye, to bury her. Funeral arrangements had to be made. When Tiffany arrived home in Dartmouth, she would have to be taken to a funeral home. We had to determine which one to use.

Arrangements had to be made with the church, which would prove to be more of a battle than we had expected. It seemed that for whichever reason, the church we wanted to use was reluctant to let me say anything about Tiffany at the service. We were told it was a decision that had been made by the archdiocese. They had determined that a eulogy was too difficult for the family. It seemed to me that if the church was about compassion, then the family should be able to grieve in their own way.

Attempting to deal with these issues, on top of our grief, while in Germany was overwhelming. Lisa's sisters again were amazing for us, doing and looking after all of these things at home. Lisa and I were left with the task of writing Tiffany's obituary. So we sat down one evening, after Kattia and Willem had gone to bed, and wrote our daughter's obituary. It was such an incredibly difficult thing to do. We had to try to put our grief aside, if only a little bit, and try to do right by Tiffany. There was so much we wanted to say but in the end, after many tears, we decided to keep it simple, the way we were sure Tiff would have preferred. Lisa and I were so proud of Tiffany. She had turned into an incredible young lady, full of kindness, compassion, and courage. Really, we wanted people to know that before anything else. We completed Tiffany's obituary and sent it home that evening, having taken yet another ugly step.

Our evenings were all spent much the same way during our time "in-between." Willem, Kattia, Lisa and I would sit at the table after the children were in bed and just talk. Even with all that the four of us were going through, those evenings were pleasant. The different topics enabled us to relinquish, if only briefly, what was the reality for us. It never lasted very long but it was pleasant while it did last. I often wonder if Willem and Kattia realized how important that was for Lisa and me, or if perhaps it was their intention to keep us all sidetracked. We drank a bit of wine during those evenings. I think we even managed a smile or two while sitting together. Our grief was front and centre but our panic and uncertainty were now gone.

I usually found a way to spend some alone time by the fire at the end of these evenings. It was time just to be by myself and reflect. Lisa or Kattia would sit up for a bit on occasion but for the most part, it would just be me sitting in front of the fire with the rest of the house in darkness.

Although Germany is loaded with cities and towns that might be considered "touristy," the industrial city of Hamm is not one of them. Very few tourists go to Hamm to do any sightseeing. As a result, the English language is not needed or used much around the city. This circumstance made it difficult for us to get detailed answers to our questions.

The most important of these questions, now, was what exactly caused Tiffany's death on that Sunday morning. The only thing we knew for absolute certain was that Tiffany did not drown. As it happens, Kattia's brother is a physician in Norway and a specialist in cold-water deaths. Norway has many cold-water fiords and a population that loves the outdoors. It made sense that he would see many such cases and he confirmed this in a conversation one evening.

He explained to me that cold-water or "reflex" death could be compared to jumping into a very cold shower or lake. When the cold water first hits the warm body, the person would gasp and inhale deeply. This shock could either lead to a heart attack or cause the esophagus to close and the victim would literally suffocate.

There are different factors that would play into the seriousness of the water's effect. Such things as water temperature, body temperature, and even body mass would all be factors in reflex death. As it happened with Tiffany, she had all of these factors working against her. She had just finished a fairly intense workout so her core temperature was higher than it normally would be. The water temperature at the time was between four and six degrees centigrade. Lastly, Tiffany was not a big girl. The doctor explained (and I believe he did not want to divulge this) that if Tiffany had tipped three or four minutes later when her body temp would have had time to come down or if she had been a bigger person, she may have walked away from the canal that day.

This was incredibly difficult to hear and only added to all the other "what ifs" we had to deal with. What if it had been teeming rain that morning? What if it had been minus ten degrees that day? Or what if it was Tiff's day to work? Any of these scenarios would have meant that Tiffany would not have been on the water that Sunday morning and that she would still be with us today. I've realized since that time that I could make myself more miserable if I were to dwell too much on the "what ifs." Nothing in the past can be changed now.

As each day in Hamm passed, arrangements began to fall into place. The timing of Tiffany's body being transported to the airport in Frankfurt for our flight home had been finalized. Our flight home had been confirmed and we knew that Tiffany would be on it. This was so important to Lisa and me – there had to be no chance we would be going home without Tiffany this time. I found over the next couple of days that this was constantly on my mind. I was so afraid that anyone could have missed a memo somewhere during the process or misinterpreted something and we would miss Tiffany.

Kattia had been making arrangements to have a small service at the canal, either at the club or at the bridge where Tiffany had disappeared. It was decided that the bridge would be a fitting place and the club was just a four- or five-minute walk away anyway. The time had been set for the late morning, a couple of days before we were to return to Canada.

Lisa and I had decided to go to the canal early just to go for a walk before the service. We parked the Smart car at the usual place at the kayak club and headed up the canal toward the bridge and the place where they eventually found Tiffany. The day brought incredibly bright, brilliant sunshine under a cloudless sky. It was cold but for the first time I could remember, there was no wind and the canal was just so calm. We walked on the downtown side of the canal this time, passing under the bridge as we walked. There was no activity as we passed. Lisa and I were pretty certain that it would only be the Sturms and a few of the club executives so there really wasn't much of a set-up involved.

We continued walking, passing under the railway pass, the health club where the dogs searched for the second time, and on toward the rail tracks farther up the waterway. We talked a bit about the previous three weeks, the things we had to do when we arrived home and how we were going to manage the days ahead. As we walked the rail tracks, we came to a small iron cross with a picture of a small boy. He had been killed by a train a few years earlier. (This young boy's cross did start the wheels in motion toward a future cross for Tiffany.) We stared across the canal to the turnaround where Tiffany was found and I thought again of how close I had been during those earlier days of searching. We also noticed the sun was quickly moving across the sky; it was time to return to the bridge for the small service.

It seemed to be growing colder now as we walked back. As we emerged from the other side of the rail pass, what we saw in the distance under the Münsterstrasse Bridge was truly amazing. There had to be a hundred and fifty people gathered at the bridge. All of these people had gathered in the cold to say goodbye to a young Canadian girl, whom many had never met, and to offer their condolences to Lisa and me.

As we walked closer, the group turned to watch us approach. Even without our Canada jackets, which had marked us in earlier days, we were recognized as being Tiffany's parents. A man walked towards us and we recognized him to be Herr Bulmer from the undertaker's. Kattia was with him and the two of them introduced Lisa and me to the priest who was to perform the service. Lisa and I were led to our place at the front of the group. I remember it was so quiet, the only sounds coming from distant cars and the water of the canal passing by just a few feet away. Just since the time that Lisa and I had begun our walk, a number of bouquets as well as a picture of our Tiff had been placed at the site.

The service was for the most part spoken in German. Upon reflection, that was fine with Lisa and me. We were well aware that this was as much for the kayak club members and the citizens of Hamm as it was for us. They were also mourning Tiffany's loss. The priest did find some room for English. Among his English offerings was this version of Henry Scott Holland's "Death Is Nothing At All":

Death is nothing.
I have only gone to the room next door.
I am I and you are you.
Everything we have been to each other, we still are.

Call me by my old familiar name;
speak to me as effortlessly as you always have.
Laugh, as you always have,
about the little jokes we enjoyed together;
Play and laugh with me,
think of me and pray for me.
Do not change the tone of your voice
and force a serious facial expression upon yourself.
Let my name be the familiar word it always was,
let it be spoken naturally,
without trace of a hanging shadow.

Life means everything it has always meant.
It remains what it has always been,
it carries on without interruption.

Why should I be out of mind, because I am out of sight?
I will wait for you,
somewhere very near,
just around the corner.
All is well.
Nothing is gone, nothing is lost.
One quick moment and everything
will be as it was before, only better,
unbelievably more happy and forever,
we will all be one in Christ.

It still surprises me a little just how much I do remember about that day. I think back to it now and it seems like a scene from a movie playing over and over in my mind. It really was a beautiful day, calm and peaceful, and bright with sunshine. It was cold, but not unbearably so. I remember Lisa's struggle and her becoming weak a number of times during the service, wanting only to collapse. I held her tight and tried the best I could to let her know I did have her and would never let her go. A number of thoughts went through my mind as we all stood there together. It was still amazing to me that Lisa and I were in the midst of all of these complete strangers, thousands of miles from our home in a strange country. But these "strangers" were here, on this day, standing in the cold to support our family.

I looked to the sky and spotted a couple of photographers on the Münsterstrasse Bridge above us. But it didn't matter to me now. They could not hurt us any more than we were hurting right now.

It was not a long service, perhaps thirty minutes or so. As he concluded the service, the priest came to Lisa and me and shook hands to offer condolences. Willem, Kattia and the three children came to us as well. And then something that we had not expected: one by one, every single person who stood there with us that day came to Lisa and me to shake hands, some to embrace us for a moment.

From five years old to eighty-five years old, all one hundred and fifty or so stood in line to offer their support. Some spoke in broken English, some were only able to speak in German, and some said nothing at all. Members of Germany's national canoe and kayak team as well as the president of their federation were there with us. One gentleman who identified himself as being from Stockholm, Sweden, told us he had read about Tiffany and kept up to date through newspapers and the Internet at home and he had flown to Hamm just for Tiff's service. We were so incredibly moved by all that these people had done for us.

After each person gave us a moment of their time, they walked to the side of the bank, to almost the exact spot where Tiffany was last seen, and dropped a single rose into the canal. Soon, there were over a hundred roses floating in the canal. When all had done so, the Sturms each did the same. Kattia then gave Lisa and me each a rose and the two of us walked over and let our roses fall from our hands into the brownish water that had stolen our daughter from us.

The current took all of the roses on their journey up the canal toward the place where Tiffany was found just a few days before. And then, the most incredible thing ... as all of the roses before ours continued to drift away from us, the two that Lisa and I had given up drifted away and then back to us again as if to say goodbye. They stayed with us for only a minute or so before leaving us again for the final time. Lisa and I stood watching our roses move away from us, and although neither of us said it, we both recognized the symbolism.

I stood with my arm around Lisa, not realizing that the group behind us was slowly breaking up. Some, I suppose, began their way home but many had started in a direction opposite the one the roses had taken and back toward the kayak club.

There was to be a small reception in the upstairs area of the clubhouse. We were in no rush to get there. We wanted to watch our roses as long as we could. Eventually, Kattia and Willem were able to motivate us toward the club to be with the group. While the boat bays of the clubhouse are somewhat cluttered with boats and equipment, making it tough to negotiate, the upstairs is a large open room with a small bar/kitchen facility off to the side. As with the clubs at home in Dartmouth, there are pictures, shelves holding trophies, old paddles, and other paddling memorabilia covering walls.

The ladies of the club had prepared some small finger foods and sweets, and tea and coffee was served. The older gentlemen of the club sat in the bar area and sipped their beverages. I watched the smaller children dart amongst the tables and the teenagers sit with their different cliques. I remember thinking that everywhere you go, things really are the same. We sat at our table, occasionally rising to thank those who came to again offer their regards. We met a few others, friends of the Sturms, and we played easily with Franz. Birgit was not feeling well and Willem did his best to comfort her without having to leave us.

Lisa and I were so grateful and a little overwhelmed by all these people had done and continued to do for us. It wasn't just that they were doing these things but the way they were doing them. These people showed us such amazing support and compassion and genuine concern for our suffering. I will never forget that.

The upstairs of the clubhouse slowly emptied and the ladies tidied up the last of the plates, cups and saucers. Lisa and I decided to take one last walk up the canal before we were to leave the following day. We thanked and said goodbye to those who were left at the club. For the most part, those who remained were the same members who had helped us with whatever we had needed.

It was late in the afternoon when Lisa and I stepped out of the club to the banks of the canal. We pulled our collars up and started back toward the bridge, the same bridge that we had stood at two hours earlier, the same bridge that had been the origin of many searches just days earlier and the same bridge where Tiffany had last been seen alive.

The sun was on its way down as we crossed the Münsterstrasse Bridge to the other side of the canal and it caused even the brown water to sparkle just a little. As we walked the path toward the turnaround, we began to catch up to the roses that had became a part of the waterway. Some were making their own way while others became tangled and travelled as a group. We walked and watched the roses as we passed. It was peaceful and quiet. There was no traffic on the opposite side of the water. The occasional rabbit crossed our path ahead of us but for the most part, it just seemed like Lisa, the rabbits and me.

We talked as we walked along but again, the panic and urgency of earlier days was gone. I thought then that the service for Tiffany was another beginning step toward some sort of closure. We had no idea then and do not know even now, as I write, when or if complete closure will ever come. I suspect that it never will and we will be treating each new day as a new step ... one day at a time for the rest of our lives.

The evening before we left for home was spent much the same way as those previous. We enjoyed a peaceful meal and a little wine as we talked. And I again sat alone in front of the fire after the others had turned in. I knew this would, in all probability, be the last time I did this and it saddened me but I wasn't sure why.

I looked again around the rooms on the main level of the house. In my mind, I could see Tiffany in the kitchen, sitting with the children at breakfast. I saw her through the dining room window, playing games with the children in the backyard. And I saw her in the entry by the back door, pushing small boots and mittens on small feet and hands, sometimes frustrated and sometimes playing and joking.

I saw Tiffany all over this house and I realized that was the reason I had this sadness inside of me. This was Tiffany's last home and it was a part of her life. It was a learning part of her life and now I was about to leave this behind as well.

BRINGING TIFFANY HOME

Tiff loved Derek and Emma immensely. Lisa and I would often catch six-year-old Tiffany in Derek's bedroom at three or four o'clock in the morning, trying to wake him up to play.

It was early in the morning and dark when we left the Sturms in their driveway for our journey home. It was so difficult this time. We did not know when we would see them again and they had been, for the past three weeks, such a huge part of our lives and everything we had gone through. More importantly, we were leaving the last place that Tiffany called home. The car that would take us to the airport in Frankfurt arrived and we stood in the driveway, both wanting and not wanting to leave. Even five-year-old Franz dragged himself out of bed to say goodbye to us, his arms around my neck not wanting to let go. I had to reassure him we would see him again very soon. The tears flowed and continued to flow after we were on our way. Lisa and I knew we would be back to Hamm soon. We had some unfinished business to attend to at the canal.

Boarding our flight was stressful. We had a difficult time confirming that Tiffany would indeed be on our flight, but we got nothing past a "we believe so." We had to rely on the information we had from Carol at home and from the undertaker in Hamm, who had informed us that Tiffany had been transported to Frankfurt early the previous evening.

The flight back to Canada was uneventful. We flew in daylight the entire way so it seemed less gloomy than perhaps it may have otherwise. Air Canada, with Brad's help I'm sure, flew us first class throughout, enabling Lisa and me to be comfortable during our flights. I recall towards the end of our flight, the senior flight attendant came to us and spoke. "I don't know how to tell you this. Your daughter is on the plane with us. She is in cargo." He was a bit unsure when we showed relief. He apparently thought we would be spooked by this information and couldn't have known that this was the way we had planned our return flight. If I recall correctly, he was so relieved at our taking this news well that he brought us a second helping of ice cream.

We had a layover of a few hours in Toronto and we called home to confirm our arrival time in Halifax. The family wanted to be there to meet us. I also spoke to Derek and he asked if I would make it home for his hockey game later that evening. I told him I would do my best. I had not seen or even thought enough about Derek and Emma the past three weeks. This must have been so hard on them. In the previous three weeks, I had only been able to spend forty hours or so at home and it was not exactly quality time. I knew I had to try to be there for them now, but I was also going to look to both Derek and Emma for strength. I knew that if it was at all possible, I would be at D's game that night.

Most of our family, along with Carol, were at the gate to meet us when we arrived. We had learned that the funeral home would also be there to take Tiffany and there was nothing for us to do as we had cleared Customs in Toronto. I made sure that Lisa was okay and then started on my way to the car to get to Derek at the rink. It was at this time that I was given more devastating news. Susan, while walking me to the car and through her own tears, informed me that while we were in Hamm, the daughter of one of our hockey parents and older sister of one of Derek's teammates had been struck and killed in a crosswalk while making her way across a busy Dartmouth street only days before.

I was shocked and the world wasn't making much sense at that particular moment. What was happening? Why were these people being stolen from us at such a young age? The entire community must be thinking the same way. And how was Derek doing in the midst of all of this? First his sister and while coping with this, a member of his hockey family. It was now more important that I get to the rink to be with Derek. This may have been more for my sake than his. I also thought back to Evelyn Hare's comment about more young people becoming victims.

Derek's game that evening was part of a major city tournament so I was aware the rink would be full of players and parents. I really had no desire to see or talk to anyone except Derek. I made my way into the rink and to the dressing room Derek's team was using. It was so good to see him and I needed that hug so badly. I was careful not to hang on too long, keeping in mind that Derek was a thirteen-year-old male and would embarrass under absolutely any circumstance. I was also able to speak with Ashley, whose sister was killed in the crosswalk. I told her that if she needed anything or if there was anything I could do for her, she could call. I thought about that afterward and just how goofy it must have sounded. I was kind of screwed up myself and don't know if I was in a position to help anyone else.

I got away from the kids and found a refuge in a small corner of the rink with my brothers and some friends and watched D's game. He seemed to play an inspired game, noticeably so according to those around me. He even managed to score the overtime goal that would win the game for his team.

It was late and I was tired when Derek and I got home from the rink. Lisa had, by then, heard about Mary-Beth and was struggling again to digest this latest bit of horror. We learned that during our first days in Hamm, Mary-Beth and her mother, Tina, were spearheading a fundraiser for Tiffany during games at different rinks. I felt incredibly helpless to return that favour to her family. I was up early the next morning to go to the Chaulks' to offer my sympathies and condolences to the family. Lisa and I attended Mary-Beth's visitation that evening and funeral the following day, knowing that the worst was still to come for us.

Lisa and I had some decisions to make about Tiffany's funeral and visitations. We first met with the directors of the funeral home. The grim task of picking out a casket as well as arrangements for visitation times and other small matters had to be taken care of.

We then met with the church. We had to discuss exactly what type of service we wanted as well as finalize the day and time of the service. Lisa also wanted the music to be just right. This proved to be difficult. We met with the church's music director but could find little to satisfy Lisa. In the end, and after again having to battle against the church's wishes, a family friend was able to convince the music director to allow Lisa's music preference.

I was beginning to become disillusioned with the church, recalling that while in Germany just days before, Lisa and I were forced to battle so that the church would allow me to say a few words at Tiffany's funeral. Now, it was something as minor as what music to play that became an issue. I am not a religious man but I do agree with much of what the church teaches with regard to basic human behaviour. But I also believe firmly, and perhaps it is just me, that any church should be compassionate in these matters and be supportive of anything that would help a grieving family through the process. It seems to me these are basic human decisions. Perhaps this ties into why so many of today's youth are turning away from the church.

Lisa and I were incredibly well looked after by our family and friends in the days before visitations and Tiffany's funeral. Outside of those first two meetings with the funeral home and church, we had only to exist. Every new detail of visitation, funeral, or anything else was looked after as soon as it arose. A neighbour or friend came to the door at what seemed to be every five minutes with food or some other necessity.

I'm not sure that the idle time was a good thing, at least not for me. Lisa wanted only to spend her time being quiet. She had to have people in the house but didn't necessarily need to be sociable. I, on the other hand, had to keep moving. I wanted to do something. I went for a few walks but for the most part, I just wandered around the house. Lisa and I were and still are different in that regard. I realize now that I chose to just wander the house because I didn't want to be away from Lisa for any length of time.

Saying Goodbye

For some unknown reason, Tiffany often made the simple act of walking seem so difficult. When we lived on the top of Celtic Drive hill, it was always a chore for Tiffany walking home. She often took a short break between steps.

The first day of visitations was Thursday, March 16. Tiffany's aunts and a couple of cousins had made up collage boards to display at the visitation. Hundreds of pictures were photocopied, carefully cut out and pasted on five poster boards. These were truly beautiful. We had pictures of Tiffany dating back to her first days after birth to just days before her death, when in Teneriefe with the Sturms. As we looked through all of these photos, we noticed the most incredible thing. Out of the hundreds of photos that were pasted on those boards, Tiffany was smiling in almost every single one of them. Whether at a family barbeque, hanging with friends, at Christmas celebrations, sitting on a horse (which was of course a given) or just sitting on her own, Tiff always had a smile on her face. That she had grown into a beautiful young woman became even more obvious in these pictures.

With the first visitation set for 7:00 p.m., we arrived at the funeral home at 6:00. Members of the family began to arrive shortly afterward. I really believed that Lisa and I were prepared for the two hours in front of us on that first evening. We had discussed the likelihood of there being many people but we could never have foreseen the actual number. That evening was a non-stop flow of well-wishers, some of whom I would never have expected to see.

Many of Tiff's friends came that evening as we had expected. But there were those present whom I had not seen in years. (Carol, a friend of my own mom's, who I had not seen in at least thirty-five years, offered Lisa and me a hug.) Some of those present were among those I never expect to see again. There were those who had never met Tiffany or Lisa and who I know wouldn't have counted me among their friends. Friends of both Derek and Emma came to the visitation to see both them and us. D and Em for the most part did their own thing. We wanted them to be comfortable and not put into a difficult situation. They spent time away from Lisa and me and the grief that it entailed and stayed close to cousins, uncles and aunts.

The first night was non-stop and I became concerned that this was too overwhelming for Lisa. But she refused to take a break away from us. She was incredibly courageous and strong. Friday, the second evening of visitation, was much the same only with an almost entirely new set of friends and well-wishers. Some of those who came through on Friday had also been with us to offer support on Thursday. Perhaps it was just a haze of grief and fatigue, but Friday evening's visitation seemed to pass more quickly than the night before and it seemed that the home emptied out quickly.

At the end of the evening, after the last guest had left and it was just the family remaining, we were told that the home would be closing Tiffany's casket forever. We were asked if there was anything we would like to give to Tiffany to have with her. I had written a letter to Tiff, reminding her of my love and the pride I had inside. And in that letter, I thanked her, in a way that would never seem adequate enough, for allowing me in her life and for teaching me all that she had. I hope now, with all that I have inside me, that she knows these things.

Derek thought for a long time about what he wanted Tiffany to have. In the end, he chose the first medal he had ever won at our national canoe/kayak championships and also the name bar from one of his hockey jerseys. It was from a jersey he had worn the season before when his team had travelled to an international tournament in Quebec. His team had played against teams from the Czech Republic and Finland, among others, and it was a special time for him.

Emma was having a very rough time coping. She found it very difficult to find something special enough for Tiffany but eventually decided on things she knew would have meaning to Tiff. She gave Tiffany her own favourite horse ornament as well as pictures that she had drawn of her and Tiff.

Lisa had written a letter to Tiffany when Tiff was just two years old, but never had the opportunity to give it to her. She had it placed with her along with a rose. Other family members had their own special things placed with Tiffany.

I have no real recollection of how we spent the two days and evenings after the visitations. Saturday and Sunday before the funeral were spent at home with the family but doing nothing in particular. Lisa's sisters were at the house, as they had been since we had arrived back home, doing what they could for Lisa, the kids and me. This did allow me some time to ponder over the words I would use in Tiffany's eulogy.

Writing Tiffany's eulogy had been a constant struggle and worry for me for days, for a number of reasons. I knew that it wasn't natural for a dad to be writing and then actually giving the eulogy at his little girl's funeral. I didn't know for certain that I would be able to get through it in front of many people. But mostly, I didn't believe that I would ever be able to do right by Tiffany. Tiffany had lived such a special life if only by the way she affected those around her. Her own kindness and caring ways, as well as her smile, were contagious. She could be counted on to do the right things. She was not a particularly competitive person, and I once commented to her on how hard she raced. Her reply: "That's what the coaches tell me to do, and what my teammates need me to do." I could never thank her enough for all that she meant to me and all that she had taught me.

I spent quite a few restless hours trying to choose the perfect words for Tiff. I wanted, or perhaps more, needed my speech to be perfect but I eventually realized that this wasn't possible. No matter what I wrote, the words looked so cold in print. I also realized, and my thoughts were confirmed by the visitations, that there were going to be many at Tiffany's funeral who had never actually met her. These people in our community, the same people who had supported our family, should be able to know a little about the young lady that Tiffany truly was. This same community had been incredibly supportive and Lisa and I knew we would never be able to thank all of these people, but we did want to at least try to let them know of our gratitude.

I believe that I finished writing, or perhaps more accurately, stopped trying to write in the wee hours of Monday morning. Tiffany's funeral was to be that afternoon. I didn't try to sleep afterwards but waited for Lisa and the kids to wake. I wanted to be awake when they got up. I knew the day was going to be so incredibly hard and wanted to be fully with them all day.

I don't know if there was much panic beforehand and I honestly do not remember if anyone came to the house before we left for the church. I know I went for a short walk around our lake during the morning. It was a day that was turning out to be remarkably similar to the day of Tiffany's first service back in Hamm. It was a day that brought incredibly bright sun under a cloudless sky. But the sun did little to help with the frigid temperature, and a biting wind made it seem even colder. The cold would eventually follow us to the cemetery later that day.

When I returned home from my walk, Lisa's mother had already arrived. She would travel with us to the church. I remember the house was quiet before a car from the funeral home arrived to pick us up. I sit here now, doing my best to find the right words to describe what we were feeling during that wait but nothing comes to mind. Perhaps that is fitting. We were numb then and I don't know that any of us actually had a concious thought.

When the car did arrive, I don't know that any of us really wanted to get in because we knew where it would take us. The driver steered his way toward the church and although I know there must have been, I don't remember seeing any people on the streets. As we got closer to the church I was, as I am sure that Lisa was, dreading the next few hours. This was still not real for us nor did it seem right to be doing this. This was not life's natural order. How were we expected to say goodbye to Tiffany?

We knew we would have support when we arrived as the family had gone ahead of us to the church. We would be the last to arrive. We also had friends who had been at the church for an hour before, handing out itineraries and preparing the reception hall. Emma had prepared a PowerPoint presentation for Tiffany, using pictures of Tiff during her growing years, and would show it, played with some of the music that Lisa had selected, during the reception at the church hall. Our nephew Eric had prepared his own special version of Tiffany's life to be played as well.

We were still quite a way from the church when we began to notice cars parked along the side of the street. And then more. It wasn't until we were much closer that we realized just how many had come to attend Tiffany's funeral. The parking lot was jammed and it took some maneuvering by our driver to get close to the church doors. It was amazing to us the number of community members who had come out that day both to remember Tiffany and to support our entire family. Even the younger friends of Derek and Emma were there to help.

As I think back now, I recall that some of the sympathy cards and notes we had received to that point, as well as more that were still to come, made reference to it taking a community to raise a child. If we really stop to think about it, there can be so many influences on a child during their growing years. Teachers, coaches, friends, teammates, clergy, the list goes on; all have some influence, at some time, over the way in which a child will grow and mature. It only goes to follow that when a child dies, there are so many people affected. The turnout at Tiffany's funeral on that cold March afternoon was confirmation of that.

There were still more people waiting to enter the church as we walked up the steps and through the front doors. The entire family was with us in the entry, including Tiff's six uncles, who were her pallbearers that day. I know that tears and hugs were plentiful amongst our family members but really, my focus was solely on Lisa, Derek and Emma. I was aware that Lisa was doing her best to try to hold it together but I also knew that she wasn't going to make it too far. I asked Derek to walk beside his mom so that she would be between us. Again, I don't know that asking that of him was fair. He was surely fighting with his own courage to make it through.

Tiffany had been brought in and was placed in front of our group. We had chosen a beautiful, light pink casket for her. It was important to Lisa that Tiffany had something soft to lie down in. I recall staring at Tiff's casket and knowing that I would do anything in this world to return Tiff to her mom's arms. I still feel very much that way today.

Our friends Cheryl and Joanie, who had come earlier to help, came out to check with us, maybe to see if we needed anything. I overheard Cheryl telling someone that all of the four hundred programs had been given out almost immediately and they were asking people to try to share. I know the church has a capacity of one thousand plus and that it was full on that day.

To be honest, I do not remember much of my own daughter's funeral from the time we entered the church. I do recall walking down the aisle behind Tiffany. I remember holding Lisa and I remember Emma having both arms around my waist as she walked. We took our seats, surrounded by family and friends, and sat through our daughter's funeral. But truly, I remember nothing about the service.

I do not recall hearing the music that Lisa had so carefully chosen, nothing of what Father Owen Connolly said. I think now that my thoughts simply went back and forth from Tiffany in the casket beside us to Lisa and my other two children who were sitting in the church pew beside me. There may have been some panic when I thought that the priest, near the end of the service, may have forgotten about my wanting to address those in attendance.

He did eventually invite me to say a few words. Although I wasn't sure if I could get through and was afraid to do this, I knew that speaking for Tiffany was something I needed to do. I wanted so badly for those present to know just a little about our Tiffy, the young lady who had been so much of their focus. It was also important to Lisa and me that our community know of our gratitude.

As I got up to walk to the microphone, I was very uncertain that my legs would carry me for even those few steps. I think now I may have looked anxious but I knew it was only my momentum that kept me from falling.

When I turned to face the congregation, it was the first time I actually realized how many were there. I took a deep breath and as I did so, I looked around. I saw many who I would have expected to see, but I think I was a bit unnerved by how many I did not recognize. I took another deep breath and was determined not to speak too quickly. As for how it turned out or how my words were received, you would have to ask someone else who was there that day because I honestly don't know. Again, to those who attended on March 20, 2006, our family is grateful. To you, Tiffy ... I hope I did okay, sweetie:

Good afternoon, and thank you all for being here with us today. I want to thank Father Owen for allowing me to say a few words.

Doing this today was important as there are some things that Lisa and I wanted to share with the people who knew Tiffany as well as the community that has held up our family over the past month. Sunday afternoon not too long ago, Derek, Lisa and I were in the kitchen. D and I were teasing Lisa about something silly, though I cannot recall now what that might have been. Emma was at the birthday party of one of her school buddies. The telephone rang and that two-minute phone call changed our lives forever. Much of what I say in the next few minutes may not be as perfectly worded as I would like or sound as perfect as I would like it to but ... no man is perfect and I'll ask you all to bear that in mind.

Tiffany died on February 19th – far from home – at the age of twenty. We, as a family, do not understand now and never will understand why this has happened. It seems so random and unfair. We have learned, however, how she died and we are able to find some comfort in some of the things we now know. We know now that Tiff was on the water in K1 with new friends – laughing, joking, and just having fun doing something she loved to do. Tiffany's death came suddenly, so quickly that we know there could not have been time to anguish or struggle with her fate. We know that her last thoughts were happy-go-lucky and carefree and we are thankful for and find comfort in that knowledge.

In looking around the room here today, I see many of Tiffany's friends as well as those of our family. And I recognize that some of you here today may not have ever met Tiffany but are here to support her family. That support is more appreciated and more comforting than we could ever say. But to those people, we would like you to know a little more about the Tiff that we know and love so very much, not just the picture that you have seen so often in recent weeks.

When going through the obvious difficulty of preparing Tiffany's obituary, Lisa and I used only one and the first adjective that came to us – Tiffany was a kind soul. Before anything else, she was that. Tiffany had great respect and great compassion for everyone or everything she came in contact with. Those are the two things that Lisa and I have tried to instill in our children before anything else – respect and compassion. And Tiffany was the perfect illustration of both of those characteristics.

Tiffany was shy – she sometimes found it difficult to make new friends. And although she had many, her circle of close friends was relatively small. But once you gained Tiff's trust and had her as a friend, you had her for life. She could be an amazing friend – supportive and loyal.

Tiffany was sometimes innocent and a bit naive but she made these traits seem truly charming and graceful. I'll always have in my memories the way Tiff crinkled her nose or put her hand over her mouth in amazement at even the smallest of life's occurrences.

She had a love of life. If you were to look through the collages that her aunts and cousins have put together, in those hundreds of pictures, you could not find a picture of Tiff not smiling.

Tiff had a number of passions but among the things she loved the most ... horses. She loved to ride, work with or just be around horses. For a number of years and even as full-time employment for a year previous to her going to Germany, Tiff was around horses. She even found a way to keep riding in Germany. The stable was Tiffy's 'feel good' place.

Tiffany was young, much too young for this to have happened. She was really still just a child, just starting to find her way. Not really knowing where life would lead her but certainly in no rush to get there. She was young and time was the one thing she had. She was just enjoying life and its new adventures and loving her family.

The one characteristic or trait of Tiffany's, however, that I will carry with me for all of my enduring time is her courage, her quiet courage. I took Tiffany overseas last summer to begin her new and year-long adventure. I met her new family and knew immediately that she would be in good hands. After spending the day, and when it was time for me to leave, Tiff and I went for a long walk. She said then, 'Dad, I'm scared' and I told her to keep looking at the big picture. She would be homesick and perhaps a bit lonely at first – but it would pass and then she could begin to enjoy this incredible life experience. And when I hugged her goodbye, I was so proud but so scared that I had tears. But I couldn't let Tiff see those tears because I didn't want her to know that I was more afraid than she was.

After Tiff's Christmas visit, when she was on her way back to her second home in Germany, I hugged her goodbye again but this time, I was so proud – and envious. Tiff was going back to a place where she truly wanted to be. A place she loved to be, doing the things that she loved to do and she couldn't wait to get there. She had so much courage just to be who she was.

I recently (in the last three weeks or so) came to the habit of going for very long walks. And during my days of searching for Tiffany along the banks of the canal — I was so aware of what I had lost but my thoughts began to shift to what in my life I had to be thankful for even though life had just dealt us the worst blow. I live in a community where people care and support each other when it is truly needed. Even thousands of miles away, Lisa and I learned of the overwhelming support for our family over this past month. It has been a more difficult time than I think anybody could possibly imagine but this community has been with us for every step. And Lisa and I felt it for every step even so far away and again — we are so grateful — and I am so thankful for that.

Tiffany spent her last eight months doing and learning new things and having the best experiences while living with a young family that Lisa and I have come to know quite well. Willem, Kattia, Anna, Franz, and Birgit gave Tiff a home filled with life and love and I am thankful for that.

My daughter Emma teaches me every day about generousity and compassion and I am thankful.

My son Derek teaches me daily that love goes far beyond words and I'm thankful.

My wife Lisa. My friend for thirty-five years and my absolute best friend for twenty. I am amazed at her strength, at her courage, and at her dignity. I want so badly to take her pain away but I don't know how. She teaches me how to be a better father, a better man and a better person. I am so thankful.

And our Tiffy — who has been teaching me about life, parenthood, patience, courage, and so much else for almost twenty years. I didn't even realize she was teaching me until she had finished. And her last lesson, with Tiffany's death, she taught me to appreciate life so much more. I am so thankful to Tiffany for all of those lessons and for twenty of the proudest years of my life.

And while Tiff may not have been the perfect daughter – I don't believe anyone is perfect – she was as close to perfect as any parent or father could hope for.

We also wanted to include a letter that Lisa had written Tiffany when Tiffany was two years old. We were advised that instead of reading the letter at the service, it might be better to include it on the funeral program. So we did. Here is a copy of it.

A letter written to Tiffany by her mother. The right time to give it to her never came. Perhaps it was meant for this day.

For My Sweet Tiffany – 1987
When I woke up this morning
The first thing I saw was your smile.
I looked into your eyes and saw them twinkle
And I knew it was meant for me.
We are all alone now and it sometimes scares me,
So I reach down into my heart
And I know that we will make it together.
Stick by my side and I promise I will never fail you.
I will love you and guide you
For as long as we have together.
Be careful of strangers that make you promises.
You will feel pain and you will suffer.
You will hurt and make mistakes.
But always remember that there are happier times ahead,
And when you find them, grab them and never let go.
For they will slip away so quickly.
These times are precious and sometimes few and far between.

You will feel joy and experience laughter.
You will love and you will succeed.
I will try to always be there for you,
But if I'm not, you should know
Everyday   You make me laugh
*   You make me smile*
*   You get me through my day*
*   You help me live.*

The following is a note that Tiffany wrote to her brother Derek on the January morning that she returned to Europe. Neither Tiff nor Derek could have possibly known that day that this was the last communication they would have with each other.

"Hey d man its me. We forgot to say goodbye to each other this morning and im not gonna be around when u get home from school. So I guess we gotta say goodbye this way. Any way have fun for the next six months in my room just remember though when i come home thats my room! Have fun playin hockey too, kick some ass, well butt for me, and be nice to emma. Im gonna miss u a bunch and i luv ya (bet u dont wanna hear that eh?). And be nice to mom and dad, theyre good people, and they luv ya too"

I know I made it back to sit with my wife and children and I'm certain I walked to them on my own but I don't remember actually taking the steps. The service concluded shortly afterward and we were soon following Tiffany out of the church. We had taken another step in the process.

126

The gymnasium where the reception was held was a mere two hundred yards or so from the church doors. Still, the car was waiting to drive us there. I remember thinking that Tiff would have gotten a kick out of that. (I still find odd, some of the things that I do recall clearly versus those things I struggle with.) I opted to have Lisa, Derek, and Emma walk the short distance with me. We entered the room and wandered toward the back not really knowing what to do with ourselves but were soon at the end of yet another receiving line where we would go through the visitation routine over again.

Perhaps it's only my own recollection and I could not comment for Lisa, but it seemed to be a bit of a lighter mood than the visitations only days earlier. Those around us were smiling and joking with each other, not like before. I didn't understand it. How could people be having those pleasant conversations while our world was being torn apart?

I got it many days later. The fact was, it was our world and not theirs. This is not to say that those people who were seemingly there to help support us were being insensitive. They were simply removed from our situation. Honestly, I had in the past been in their place when the death of a friend hadn't greatly affected my world, only that of the family suffering the loss.

Maybe it was exhaustion or the fog that had enveloped me throughout the funeral service. It just seemed there was so much small talk or some simply standing in front of Lisa and me, not knowing what to say. I couldn't deal with that. I was not able to simply stand in front of someone and say nothing. I was emotionally and physically tired. My legs were getting weak from standing.

I remember seeing Derek across the gym and wanting to go hug him. He has been my hero since the very moment that he was born and he still is.

Emma's and Eric's PowerPoint presentations were showing on the wall behind Lisa and me. Emma, however, was nowhere to be seen and I began to panic. She was struggling with losing Tiffany and now she was having to endure so much attention and confusion. We were going to be leaving for the cemetery soon. I found her with her cousins. Not wanting to be around anyone whom she didn't know well, she had found her refuge with those she trusted.

It was some time before the room would be empty. There were only family members and a few closer friends left when it was time to leave for the interment. I didn't want to go. I would have done anything to avoid going to that cold cemetery. No parent ever wants to see their child put in the ground. So it only followed that the drive from the church to the cemetery seemed to take very little time. I tried my best to convince myself that it was only Tiffany's shell we were about to put into the ground and that her soul was, and still is, free and everywhere around us. Even now, it is that thought that helps to keep me going from day to day.

We were not at the cemetery long. All in all, with the interment itself, it took about ten minutes to put an end to what had been twenty incredibly wonderful years. Tiffany's casket had arrived before us and was prepared to be lowered. Lisa, Derek, Emma, I and a few others placed roses on the top. As I placed my rose on her casket, I whispered a soft goodbye and again reminded Tiff how much I loved her but it didn't seem like enough.

I returned to Lisa. On the exterior, she appeared so courageous but inside she was being ripped apart. When she wasn't focused on Tiffany's casket in front of her, she only stared ahead. But her stare was blank, as if she were looking through people and oblivious to anybody or anything around her.

We didn't stand long. Our family returned to the car leaving those who had gathered there … and Tiffany. We did not want to see the casket lowered. That's the way we left it as we drove away. We simply left Tiffany's shell to be given up to the earth at the same time hoping that her soul, her essence, was still all around us. I don't recall any words, if any, that may have been spoken on the drive home.

It wasn't long before family and close friends began to arrive at our home. I tried for what may have been all of two minutes to be a gracious host. I then took a seat at the kitchen table and poured the first of a few rums. Guests would have to fend for themselves. I sat in my own little world for a bit.

I remember thinking briefly about my mom. She had once told my brothers and me that she hoped she would die before we did because she wouldn't be able to handle losing us. This caused me to think that she was much wiser than her young age should have allowed.

For the most part, it was only a few of the guys, brother Mike and brothers-in-law, sitting at the table. I wanted to go to Lisa in the next room but that would have meant I would have had to talk with people. Lisa's sisters came through to update me on what or how she was doing.

I knew Lisa. I was thinking that she really didn't want to be social either but at the same time didn't want to be alone in a quiet house. The kids and I would be there, of course, but we were all in the same emotional state, not able to help each other much. Inevitably, the house slowly emptied. Some family stayed into the evening but we were eventually left to fend for ourselves for the night. Exhaustion and wanting so badly to escape consciousness helped with some restless sleep.

THE MONTHS AFTERWARD

*For a time, Tiff's bedroom was in the basement of
our home. She would too often be there with her
door closed, shut out from the rest of the world.
Eventually, Lisa and I removed her bedroom door,
if only to compel her to be available to us when we
called to her. We thought this had made our point.
When the door was returned, so was the routine.*

I n many ways, the next day was the real beginning of
the rest of our lives. Support was still there, of course.
Friends and neighbours continued to drop by with prepared meals or other needs. Cards and best wishes still
arrived by mail and sometimes telephone. Lisa's family
continued to be a wall of support. But in truth, all of this
would not get us what we ultimately wanted, or more to
the point, needed. We needed to have Tiff back. Nothing
else. We are and will always be so incredibly grateful for
all that our community has done for us but this is our reality. I'm fairly confident that any grieving parent would

tell you the same. It was all that Lisa and I could do to simply exist from day to day for many weeks and then months afterward.

Derek and Emma seemed to be at least coping, considering what they had been through. I know that kids deal with their grief differently than adults. It was explained to me once that children cope with their grief as if carrying a large stone. It weighs heavy until a distraction comes along, a hockey game perhaps. Children are able to put aside their grief, or stone, until whichever particular distraction is gone and it is time to pick it up again.

Derek still wasn't saying much but there were no obvious or drastic changes in his disposition. He had also just recently turned thirteen so it was difficult to tell which mood changes were related to Tiffany's loss and which were just part of becoming a teenager. For the longest time, I would watch D's body language. When he looked as if he might be struggling, I would talk with him to try to know for sure.

Emma was having a much more difficult time. She cried herself to sleep every night. She set up a little corner of her room with her own small memorial to Tiffany. She prayed for Tiffy every night there and it seemed to make her feel better, still close to Tiff. Her friends were supportive even for their young age. When she did return to school, however, there would still be many days when I would pick her up and bring her home because she simply couldn't make it through.

Days like this made things so much more difficult. Neither Lisa nor I could find any parenting skills within ourselves. Paying bills was risky because I really wasn't capable or caring enough to even know what I was paying. Grocery orders were kept to a minimum, partly because

I just wasn't up to it and partly because I didn't want to risk meeting anyone and having to have a conversation.

I suppose things may have been easier (if possible) for me than they were for Lisa in that I tried to be so focused on looking after her and the kids. I tried to be the rock Lisa needed me to be, to be supportive and protective. I got D to hockey and did my best to be the dad he needed and the one he had been missing. I did my best to be strong for Emma and answer all the questions she had and to comfort her. So I tried to throw myself into all of these roles: husband, parent, payer of the bills, psychiatrist, and so on.

I even decided to return to coaching in May. Ironic that I was attempting to lose myself in the very sport that took our daughter from us. Our family had always had a passion for the sport of sprint canoe (which is why Tiffany was on the water in Germany) and I had always been at home there. I was fairly confident that doing these things would be both distracting and therapeutic. While attempting to get away from the grieving process, though, I was almost purposely avoiding it, something that I would pay for later.

As a family, we were still in existence mode. It was, for the most part, all we could do to get through our days. We spoke to a few different doctors in an attempt to get a grip on the grieving process. It was confirmed, at least for me, that there is no set grieving process. With regard to when, how strongly, or perhaps even if a parent recognizes different aspects of grief, I think that everyone is different. For those first months, I was probably in a bit of denial but even now I really don't know. Maybe months of numbness. Again, I really don't know.

I was still so aware of the days on my own on the banks of the canal in Hamm. During the seventeen days that Tiffany was missing, I had experiences that have changed who I am forever – a person cannot endure these things and not be affected. I do not, even for a moment, regret staying behind to search for Tiffy. I know that I would have regretted coming home when Lisa did.

It's just that it was so difficult. Those days were a constant in my thoughts and visions. There were still things that were haunting me, in particular the evening when I was sure that I had found Tiffany. There were things I knew I had done but they still didn't seem real. I was so unsure of myself that I didn't want to talk to anyone about anything. I know I did consider speaking to Susan just to find out what she might remember about our phone conversation that evening but I didn't do that, thinking she may tell Lisa, adding to her misery.

So all of these things were contributing to my own poor state of mental, and so physical, well-being. I honestly believed I would be able to handle things. Perhaps for a while I did and it was just my own grieving process at work. I believe that I was in a much worse place a year after, and even now almost two years later, than I was in those first months.

I don't know for sure if there are things that we felt we should or in some cases, had, to do. Tiffany's twenty-first birthday was approaching. Lisa wanted to do something as a family to acknowledge it. A friend gave us the use of his beach cottage on Prince Edward Island for a few days. We thought this would be a quiet time we could spend together as a family and to remember Tiff.

Lisa, the kids, and I made the four-hour drive one evening and arrived, convinced that our being together was what we should be doing. I suppose the idea, in theory, was a good one but it turned out to be unworkable. Derek and Emma were bored (mostly, I think, because Lisa and I were not particularly entertaining). Lisa and I discovered very early the next morning that our comfort zone was really to be around familiar things – Tiffany's things. We packed up and returned home by early afternoon, having learned to take another small step.

I had mentioned that on our return trip to Hamm, Lisa and I had wandered through shops during our days of waiting. It was during one of our morning outings that we came across a display of Tiffany's "human baskets." At that time, we had taken the address and actual terminology for these things. Called *strandkorbe* in Germany, they are essentially closed-in reclining beach chairs, often made out of wicker – the cadillac of beach chairs, if you will. Tiffany had discovered them while vacationing with the Sturms on the northern German island of Juist, and she spoke of them with exuberance during her Christmas visit. They were available from different manufacturers within Germany.

Once home we were able to find a company who, once overcoming the language barrier, was able to provide us the shipping information we required to have our *strandkorbe* sent. We chose an attractive brown wicker basket with a blue and green striped cushion seat and back and looked forward to its delivery. As Tiffany's birthday was approaching, it was our hope it would arrive in time for that occasion.

As I think back now, it was a sort of bizarre thing – waiting for Tiffy's chair. We were in a place where time actually seemed to be standing still but at the same time, Lisa and I actually looked forward to the delivery. Our "basket" arrived shortly after Tiff's birthday and it has been, in an extraordinary way, a place where Lisa and I can sit together, and find great comfort. In the best way, it is as if we are able to sit with Tiff and when alone, it is a place to just talk with her.

Lisa and I remained in close contact with the Sturms in Germany. We had shared so much with them, including one of our three most prized possessions: Tiffany. And Kattia and Willem had shared their lives and their children with Tiffany as well. Kattia and Willem informed us they had made plans to come to Nova Scotia, with the children, to spend several weeks during June and into July, only four months after Tiffany passed. They would be with us for a few days, then tour the province before returning to be with us for four or so more days.

I wasn't sure how this would sit with Lisa. Might it be just too overwhelming for her or perhaps go the other way and enable her to be busy or distracted? Kattia and Willem had been so good to us during our time with them when Tiff had been missing and subsequently were there to bring Tiffany home. We had become close and appreciative of each other during our evenings at their dining room table back in Hamm and genuinely enjoyed their company. I also learned that, in terms of the way that our separate families were put together (I had married into Tiffy and Willem had married into Anna), we were quite similar. And I very much looked forward to being with Anna, Franz, and Birgit even if the only reason was that it was an opportunity to look after them for a bit, just as Tiff did. It was an opportunity to perhaps know them as Tiffany had and I looked forward to that.

We did what we could to prepare for the Sturm family. Derek and Em actually agreed to share a room during their visit in order to accommodate them. Preparations, even though minor, gave Lisa at least a short-term goal. She bought new towels and linens, cleaned everything in the house (some things twice) and stocked the fridge with groceries. This was an important time for Lisa. I think it gave her a distraction when she needed one most.

The Sturms arrived shortly after supper on a warm June evening and took the Halifax International Airport by storm. There was a whirlwind of luggage, car seats, and Franz and Birgit seemingly everywhere at the same time. To this day, I don't know how Willem and Kattia managed the crossing. I keep in mind that they were still dealing with all that had happened in the last few months. Between their rented van and our car, we got everybody to our home safely. Exausted, the children went to sleep easily, enabling us to catch up with Willem and Kattia for just a little bit before we all called it a night.

Up early the next morning, five-year-old Franz was already at work cleaning my backyard. Within an hour or so, he had all of the dead branches, debris and such from a winter's worth of storms stacked neatly in a pile at the very back of the yard and was looking for more to do. So, if in ten or so years time, you happen to be looking for an extraordinarily motivated, hard-working, and hard-headed German lad to employ, have I got the perfect candidate for you.

It was mid-morning, after we had all eaten and spent a little more time catching up, that I found Lisa alone up-stairs in our bedroom. She had been crying. This was not surprising as spending much time crying had recently be-come a part of everyday life. This seeemed a little differ-ent and I immediately thought that my fears were coming to life. Was Lisa just too overwhelmed by the visit? Was the loss of Tiffany all that she could see, which of course was understandable? It was only when I saw what Lisa was holding in her hands that I knew what had her so churned up. All I could do was to sit with her.

I recognized what she held in her hands immediately, even though I had never seen them before. Kattia had taken Lisa aside moments earlier and given her a package she had brought from the police in Hamm. In it was the clothing that Tiffany had been wearing at the time she went missing on February 19, the exact clothing that Tiffany had been wearing when she died.

It was more than I could deal with at that moment. These items of clothing that immediately became so important to us were still covered with brown stains from the silt at the bottom of the Datteln-Hamm canal. There were small tears in places, from the underwater journey from where she disappeared to where she would eventually be found. The autopsty report that we would have translated later would match postmortem injuries with locations of those tears and rips in Tiff's clothing.

Even now, on some evenings while alone, I will hold these items of clothing, still unwashed, in a vain attempt to get close to Tiff. As I reread this last sentence, I realize how strange it must sound. But really, there is no normal way to grieve.

Lisa and I sat on the edge of the bed for a little while afterward and let the world pass by us just a little more. Our guests, as well as D and Em, would have to do without us for just a bit.

Even with the addition of Tiffany's clothes adding to our already existing pain, spending time with Franz and Birgit over the next couple of days was a nice place to be. Franz and I played on the floor with some of Derek's old toys and he declared himself, without actually verbalizing the idea, mayor/leader/king of our small, imaginary town. Apparently, at least in Franz's world, the head of the town not only gets to drive the best cars, he drives all of the cars … and at the same time.

Birgit then insisted on going with me on a shopping excursion. This was a most pleasurable and amusing experience. We met a number of my friends and acquaintances that morning and most did their best to befriend Birgit. She, however, would have none of it. She was certainly not intimidated by anyone new. She simply chose to stare at these new acquaintences and say absolutely nothing.

Anna and Emma became fast friends, helped along by Anna's understanding of basic English. The two became a fixture at our canoe club and because Tiffany had introduced her to sprint kayak at her home in Hamm, Anna was able to fit in immediately. Anna would spend time with us after Kattia and Willem returned to Germany days later.

We managed to keep a light mood when the Sturms were with us, even with all that was hanging over us. World Cup soccer was in full swing, and Derek and I introduced Willem to our own version of sport mayhem. The last of the Stanley Cup finals were also going on and D and I enjoyed the benefits of Willem's analytical mind. Some time was spent on the Halifax waterfront, where a tour allowed for a brief education in Halifax's history.

The Sturms also got their first taste of Nova Scotia lobster, vastly different from what they were used to in Germany. Birgit had her first stare-down with a lobster that was almost her size. "Victory or death!" Glad to report that even an already cooked lobster was no match for

Birgit's no-blink intimidation. For his part, Franz was not waiting for the conclusion of Birgit's battle. Butter knife, and whatever other weapon, in hand (he may have used his shoe at one point) he only wanted to eat. Just as well. If it wasn't the lobster in front of him, it would have been almost anything else ... no shortage of appetite.

Even with all the "festivity" it was obvious, at least to us grown-ups, that we were only hanging on. There was a very large part of our family's existence missing. Nobody spoke of her much, which is not to say she was never brought up, but Tiffany was always on everyone's mind. In private, tears were shed. We would sit in silence. Tiffany's absence, her death, was really all there was. Everything else was just a mask.

It was difficult to say goodbye to the Sturms on the day they left, even though we knew we would see them again in just six weeks. Lisa and I had already made arrangements to travel to Europe, and Hamm, with D and Em. We still had our "unfinished" business at the canal. Anna stayed with us for a few days more before spending time with another former nanny, who would take her back to Hamm.

I did go back to coaching for the summer, thinking it might actually be a bit therapeutic. My group was so understanding but for me, the effort was a disaster. I remember one evening, an attempt to explain a technique was followed only seconds later by my turning to one in the group and asking, "What did I just say?" There were many sessions like that. Things like that do not do much to instill confidence in any athlete. Most evenings, I really felt like I was robbing these people, but they were patient. As I think back now, they were probably there more for me than the other way around. As I sit and write today, I am still a sprint canoe coach of sorts, though I know my days as one are winding down.

Lisa and I are, as well as husband and wife, best friends. And because we have been so for almost forty years, we have begun to take on some similar traits and thinkings. (We agree more and more these days on the parenting of our children.) However, one difference between us is that Lisa has a much more analytical mind than I do. Even with Tiffany's death, I was only trying to deal with the "it is what it is" element. For my part, I needed to try to cope with what was in front of us, which was difficult enough. Lisa pushed for more.

So when Tiffany's autopsy report arrived from the coroner in Hamm, via their police department, Lisa was determined to have the report translated into something that we could understand. Make no mistake about it, I was on board every step of the way. Whatever Lisa felt she needed to do or have to try to get to a better place, or to get on the road to a better place, I would do anything to get her there. This still is now, and always will be, my priority.

I had already spoken to a specialist in Norway about "reflex death" and had just a little insight. The autopsy, we were sure, would provide more detailed information about Tiffany's death, the exact cause, any other injuries both while still living and postmortem, and so on. Lisa would tell me many months later that she really wanted to know everything she possibly could about the time between Tiffany's disappearance and the time that her body was recovered. She said she wanted to know what happened to Tiffany during the seventeen days she was missing.

I didn't understand her statement on a couple of different levels. I was certain that such things could never be known for certain. Tiffany's two-kilometre journey may have been completed in seventeen days or seventeen hours; there is no way to know.

But it was more the "why" she had to know that bothered me. Lisa tried to explain to me that it was a mother thing, perhaps her way of being with Tiffany when Tiff needed her most. It is something that I won't even pretend to understand. Even with all of her insistence, I still felt very sure that Lisa really only needed one answer. She needed to know, for absolute certain, that Tiffany did not suffer. That Tiffany did not have any anguish in her last moments.

I believed that already, mostly because I had the benefit of speaking to the doctor in Norway and partly, I suppose, because I just wanted so badly to believe it. I was confident enough to include this in the eulogy I had written for Tiffany. I guess Lisa needed more scientific information.

We soon found out that having an autopsy, or just about anything else, translated from German to English is not an easy process. Apparently, the languages do not mesh very well, especially when attempting to translate medical phrases and terminologies. Through a friend we were able to arrange an appointment with a physician, of German heritage, in Halifax. He was a gracious man and we so much appreciated his time with us.

I think Lisa and I both felt the same about our meeting from the very moment we entered his office. On an overcast and chilly day, we travelled to our meeting hoping for just a few answers and some comfort. And I suppose we did get some of what we needed, just not in the detail we needed it. But as I think back now, the doctor seemed hesitant to be graphic in any way about the information contained in the autopsy. I really believe now that he was trying to protect us from any horrors. But in his attempt, he left us wondering if we had understood him correctly. I don't know … perhaps this is only my recollection now. I do know that neither Lisa nor I was very cognizant of anything in those early days.

In a conversation with Chistina Hoehne weeks later, she agreed to take the autopsy report with her to Germany where she was going to visit with her father. He, by chance, was a retired physician. Really, his translation confirmed what we needed to hear: the exact cause of Tiffany's death in medical terms and that there were no underlying causes in her death such as a heart problem. We were also able to learn that injuries on Tiffany's body were inflicted postmortem. This was further confirmation that Tiff, in all likelihood, did not struggle with her fate.

There was to be a subsequent or a follow-up to the original autopsy report but we never did recieve it from the coroner in Hamm. And we didn't need it. This would have confirmed that Tiffany was not under the influence of drugs or alcohol at the time of her accident. Lisa and I already knew the answers to those questions. Anyone who has ever met Tiff would also know these answers.

When Lisa and I had gone for our long walk prior to the March service in Hamm, we had come across a small iron cross by the rail tracks. It was a marker for a young boy who had died there a few years before. We knew then we would do this same thing for Tiffany. We knew we would be back in Hamm, and sooner rather than later, to put our marker for Tiffany somewhere along the banks of the canal.

That time came in August, seven months after Tiff's death. Because of the difficulty of getting through our days immediately after Tiffany's funeral, Lisa and I were not emotionally able to research the type of marker we thought Tiff would like and, subsequently, a manufacturer for what we needed. Lisa's sister Susan came to our rescue. She researched manufacturers of iron, granite and other types of markers. She was able to find out which design types might fit best for us.

Eventually, we were left with only a couple of names to ponder over. There was one man named Fred Baltzer, who lived and worked in Nova Scotia's Annapolis Valley, who came to visit with Lisa and me at our home during this process. We were impressed with this man's caring nature and genuine sincerity when he sat with us. He told us at that first meeting that he had felt connected to Tiffany and to her story. (We would learn later that Fred had a connection to Germany as well.) We knew before Fred got up from our kitchen table that he would be the man to create what we needed.

Lisa and I had sketched a design and dimensions, a one-inch-thick galvanized iron cross that would be split in a fleur-de-lys fashion at the cross ends and top. Fred would hollow out two areas of the cross for us. A six-inch-tall oval, to accommodate a granite picture of Tiffany, would sit just under a smaller square plaque containing Tiffany's birth date as well as her date of death. Trusting our then fallible instincts proved to be absolutely the correct decision.

On a damp day in June, I made the one-hour drive to Fred's rural Annapolis Valley home to pick up the sixty-pound iron cross he had made for Tiffany. I was pleased at how it turned out. It was exactly how Lisa and I had envisioned it.

We still had not settled on a place to erect Tiffany's monument in Hamm. The canal bank at the immediate spot where Tiffany had gone in the water was almost directly under the Münsterstrasse Bridge. This area was sometimes populated by questionable characters during the warmer months. A temporary plaque I mounted under the bridge, along with a personal letter to Tiffany, before I returned home the first time had soon been stolen. Lisa and I felt that anything we put at that location for Tiff would have a short lifespan.

We considered the area at the barge turnaround, the area where Tiffany's body had been found, but thought it too far removed and not very accessible to the walking public.

The area of the canal where Tiffany had gone in the water is only thirty metres or so wide. On the opposite side of the canal from the bridge location, there is a walking path that is a relatively open space. The more we thought about it, the more sense it made to erect Tiff's cross there. This exact spot was less than forty metres from where Tiffany had last been seen alive.

We still had not received permission from the city of Hamm to put Tiff's cross in the ground anywhere. Although this is not necessarily a good trait to have, I have always been one to buck the system. I think it goes to my "you don't have to be a pilot to recognize a plane crash" mentality. If it's the right thing to do, well, I guess we try to do that right thing.

To me, it was a no-brainer that Lisa, Derek, Emma, and I would go to Hamm and erect Tiffany's cross … permission or not. What would they do? Would they make us remove it? I was sure that, based on what I knew, the citizens of Hamm would revolt. Surely, things would be fine when we arrived in Hamm.

Our family left for Europe in August, Tiffany's sixty-pound, split at the ends, fleur-de-lys, five-foot cross (half of which would be in the ground) in tow. Because we would travel for a week or so before arriving in Hamm, our cross would be a constant companion with our luggage for a while.

The pre-Hamm part of our trip was not without a specific itinerary. Tiffany and I had done some fun things and visited some magical places only one year before, when we were on our way to meet the Sturms in June. Since Lisa and I were still not capable of formulating a well-thought-out plan, we chose to have history decide exactly where we would go. The four of us would retrace the footsteps Tiff and I had taken during our own tour.

We landed in Frankfurt and headed our rented Volkswagen on the one-hundred-and-eighty-five-kilometre drive to the small historic village of Rothenburg ob der Tauber in central Germany. Tiffany and I had spent a couple of days there after, and I am ashamed to say it now, discovering it while looking for a place to crash after a day of driving.

Historic Rothenburg is a walled town, built as a fortress on the Tauber River centuries ago. The town is complete with cobblestoned streets, horse-drawn wagons and incredible Gothic and Baroque achitecture. The town was an important destination for artists during the Romantic period of German art. A complete tragedy was avoided when Allied bombardments on March 31, 1945, destroyed only the eastern section of the old town, leaving the historical section intact. The ruined areas were later rebuilt "according to medieval plans."

We found accomodation in the same inn where Tiffany and I had stayed. The next day we wandered the streets and fortress walls. It was nice family time and I would share the things that Tiff and I had done with Lisa, Derek, and Em. We visited the same shops, strolled the same small streets, and of course took photos of the same horses.

The first days of our trip would set the tone for the rest of our European tour. We were able to smile and laugh a bit, things we hadn't done since Tiffany's death. We ate supper at the same restaurant, outside the walls of the town, and I was able to tell the kids that Tiff became hooked on the music videos that were spewing out of the televisions mounted on the walls.

Our next stop was Munich and Lisa and I both knew this would go one way or the other. We had shared time here as a family only a few years before and it was terrific time together. Now here we were, trying to have a family vacation but without Tiffany. Our hotel was a short distance from both the *hofbanhauf* (train station) and the small hostel where Tiff and I had stayed.

Much of the twenty-minute walk to the Marienplatz, a historic town square in the middle of the city, and farther on to our favourite beer hall/eatery, the Hofbrauhaus, was familiar to Lisa and the kids. It was still kind of mind-boggling to me that Tiffany was able to maneuver herself and me back to our hostel after we had perhaps too many beers at the Hofbrauhaus on our first night in Europe a year ago.

I have often said, only half jokingly, that the Hofbrauhaus is my favourite place on earth. When you walk through the doors, it is like coming home. Although it's

147

the many types of delicious German beers that are its draw, the Hofbrauhaus also offers an assortment of pub-quality meals – if you're into Bratwurst and pig's knuckles. My children were not. Knowing that Tiff and I had spent a fun evening here not long ago even managed to put a smile on my face if only for just a moment. The hall starts to populate itself after the supper hour and eventually becomes one big party, not unlike a pub at home in Halifax-Dartmouth. The difference is that at a beer hall in Munich, instead of meeting and speaking with someone from around your town, you're hanging out and partying with people from around the world.

The four of us sat at the same table that Tiff and I had, a theme that would follow us throughout the week. I told Lisa and the kids about the various people Tiff and I had met, including one shit-housed young American fellow who insisted that he and Tiff be married right away. After a beer at my home away from home we walked slowly back to our hotel.

We treated Derek and Em to a meal at what is supposed to be one of the most active McDonald's in Europe. Not totally inconcievable considering Munich's status as Germany's third largest city. Imagine three floors of kids toting skateboards and eating Big Macs. Lisa and the kids were tired and chose to settle in for the evening. Still jet-lagged, we had also done quite a bit of walking over the past two days. I was too wound up to sleep so I opted to go for a walk. After buying a couple of beers at a corner store, I wandered some of the streets of Munich for a while.

I suppose that the Munich portion of our trip would be considered a success of sorts. We were able to talk about Tiff a bit and smile at the same time, although I certainly had no expectation that this would be our norm in the weeks and months to come. After a nice breakfast in the hotel dining room the following morning, we made the drive to Prague.

With its stunning achitecture, historical areas and buildings, everyone in the world should have an oppotunity to visit this magical city. I am so glad I was able to share it with Tiff. Again, we were able to stay in the same building Tiff and I had stayed in. We spent our evenings in an incredibly large apartment just across the hall from the one she and I had shared. We walked the streets of both the old town and the new.

Once more, the four of us shared the things Tiffany and I had. Derek and I laughed as Lisa and Emma wrestled each other for the right to sit in the exact chair Tiffany had sat in at a pizza parlour. We people-watched from the same bench that Tiff and I had sat at in front of the Tyne Church in the city square. Lisa spent lots of Euros in the same shops. I told the kids how I had gotten Tiff to sit on the hood of a Ferrari while I took her picture and how we ran like stink afterwards for fear of getting caught by the owner. As in Munich, we were able to smile at our memories and stories of Tiffany. But we knew we would be finishing in Hamm in the following days and they would be difficult.

We arrived at the Sturms' toward the end of our European tour, after our stops in the other cities that Tiffy and I had shared. We sat with Kattia and Willem while Franz and Birgit, in their youthful enthusiasm, crawled over Derek and Emma.

Eventually, Lisa and I did take D and Em to the canal, to the place where their sister died. It was incredibly difficult to be there. Obviously, it brought some terrible memories back, of the days and the nights that Lisa and I had spent while Tiffany was missing. But it was also difficult to watch Derek and Emma try to cope with being here for the first time. Derek had not shown much emotion before this. But now, after seeing the exact place, he did break down and I will admit that I was relieved. He was grieving and he needed to. Derek would tell me through tears that he couldn't understand how something like Tiffany's accident could happen in such a small place and how nobody could have seen anything. Emma remained quiet and only asked questions, also through her tears, as they came to her.

We all made the walk to the place where Tiffany had eventually been found. We didn't speak. Lisa, Derek, and I watched as Emma picked flowers and threw them into the water for Tiffany. It was warm and sunny, just as Lisa and I had hoped. We sat for quite a while, separate but together at the same time, still not talking much. We just sat, and thought, and remembered.

We travelled to the canal the day after our arrival in Hamm to add Tiffany's memory to the water's edge, still without permission from the city of Hamm to do so.

Kattia's father owns a landscaping company, so she had made arrangements to have concrete mix, shovels, and other necessities on hand prior to our arrival in Hamm. I had thought to bring a level, stakes, string and some other requirements from home. As Kattia had been the most involved with attempting to gain this permission (again, the language issue), I sensed she was frustrated but didn't want to recommend proceeding with such a rebellious act anyway. But I have lots of experience in being an idiot when making decisions of this sort.

We had received a letter of condolence from the city's mayor so I couldn't fathom a problem on his end. I was absolutely certain that every single police officer, firefighter, rescue worker, diver – anyone who had any involvement in the search for Tiffany – would favour our plan. None of that mattered, of course. I was putting a cross up ... and I was doing it that day. The day was sunny and warm and because it was a Sunday, the downtown area was for the most part quiet. Of course, we wanted the Sturms to be a part of this event with us if it was comfortable for them and the children in particular.

Once at the canal, Lisa and I chose a location along the walking path within six or so feet of the water's edge. Because there was no growth in the water here, we thought it nice that Tiff's clubmates would be able to see the cross as they passed it on the water.

As I set to work digging the hole, our mood wasn't too terribly somber. I think perhaps the best way to describe it would be just a quiet celebration for Tiffany. Very soon after I started to dig, the strangest thing occurred – people started to show up. Some were Kattia's family members. Some were club members or executives of Tiff's kayak club. I remember clearly, even now, looking up at one point to see Marcus walking towards us. Heck, if we had a cop with us now, we must be good to go.

I didn't say much as I worked and I don't even know if I was aware of others' conversation. Every so often, Lisa or Derek or Em ... or Franz ... or Birgit ... would take a turn bringing dirt out of the hole. I am sure that if left to him, five-year-old Franz would do everything on his own. Slowly, things got done. Hole dug, cross placed in the ground, plumbed and levelled and cement poured.

Everyone seemed to become more involved after that point and I was glad for it. I know it would have been more than selfish of me to do all of it on my own; others wanted their opportunity to do something for Tiff as well. So when my part was done and it was time for the other things to be done – ornaments and letters to be buried in the wet cement as well as flowers arranged around the base of the cross – I walked up to a small elevation only twenty metres away … and totally lost it.

It seemed to come out of nowhere to hit me all at once. I looked across the canal, not even a stone's throw from where Tiffany had gone in the water that day. My gaze went only one hunderd metres up the water, to where the cadaver dogs and divers had searched for Tiffany in the water on that cold February day. I started bawling like a child. Morrie Schwartz (*Tuesdays With Morrie*) said it was okay for guys to cry and I had been subscribing to that idea plenty in the previous six months. I don't know if I had any specific feelings or if I know for sure what it was that overwhelmed me, but I suspect any decent doctor could take a pretty good hack at it. Kattia walked up the bank to me a short time later. We didn't say anything to each other. She only sat down next to me and we hurt together. Sometimes, life just sucks.

Once all the flowers were laid and candles lit, a member of the club executive said a prayer in German. It was such a nice tribute to Tiffany. Those few executives of Tiff's kayak club invited us all back to the clubhouse for a small snack when we were done at the canal. I really didn't care for a lot of attention at that time but once I learned that Germany was holding its national sprint championships elsewhere and the club would be deserted, I agreed to go along. The people in the Hamm club had been so incredible for us and had done everything they could to help. If we needed anything from them in their capacity, all we had to do was ask. They are special people to us.

There really were no expectations going into our trip to Europe and putting a marker for Tiffany at the canal. It had plenty of potential to be a complete disaster and just too emotionally difficult. As with anything else we had tried, or will try in the future, to do for Tiffany, we didn't know how painful it might be.

I was sure that I wanted Derek and Emma to see the place where Tiffany had died. I didn't want Germany to be just a cold place that stole their sister from them. And I wanted them to see it when it was sunny and warm and a pleasant place to be. This would be unlike the damp and the cold and the misery that Lisa and I had dealt with only six months earlier.

I was also sure that I needed to put a marker at the canal for Tiffany. It was important, perhaps more to me than anyone else, that Tiffany be remembered in Hamm. She had made her life there and grown so much. Hamm had become a very important part of her growing years. She had begun to learn independence here. But I didn't know what impact the trip would have, especially since we had specific other purposes for coming.

We returned home to Dartmouth having taken yet another step. This step was huge, though, for a number of different reasons. We were able to get Derek and Emma to the place where Tiffany had died. As difficult as it was for them, they now knew all they had to know about what had happened on February 19, 2006. We, as a family, were able to talk about Tiffany and remember her with a smile, although this would not be as easily done in times to come. Lastly, I was able to put a marker at the canal for Tiff. She would not be forgotten in Hamm and a piece of her would remain there, in the place that had become so important to her, the place where she had started to learn independence.

TIFFANY FROM BEYOND

Tiffany has always been just a bit stubborn. Even as a four-year-old, after hearing that it was not yet time to have her hair cut, she decided to cut it herself. The result was less than spectacular.

I honestly did hesitate to add the following paragraphs to this book. Eventually, I realized it would be insulting to any reader to not let them make up their own mind about a possible life after death. I can only tell you of some of my own experiences since Tiff's death. For any reader who may not believe in an afterlife or who may not be in any way spiritual, you may prefer to skip ahead a few pages.

Only three years ago, I may have been a page jumper as well. In the last two years, however, I have had reason to change my thinking. I certainly do not consider myself to be more, or at all, religious, but I do now consider myself to be more spiritual. For as long as I can remember, I have seen things or had experiences that I could not explain. Certainly, I have discussed these things with very few people for fear they would think I was nuts.

On the morning of March 8, 2006, my daughter Tiffany stood in front of me in our family room. This was seventeen days after her death. She stood there as plainly as you or me for as long as five or six full seconds. I can tell you even now just what she was wearing and about the apologetic look on her face, the "Dad, I messed up" look. Of course, Tiffany had been deceased for more than two weeks by then. So was that experience real on that morning? I may have doubted it had it not been for what has happened since.

Not long after Tiffany's funeral, less than a month I think, I was lying in bed hoping to find some sleep when I became aware of a television or a radio left on somewhere in the house. This wasn't surprising as I had two children who were at that age. My motivation levels were still very low so rather than get up to find the source, I chose to simply listen to it.

I did begin to get uptight when this happened a second and then a third evening and challenged D and Em on their neglect one morning at breakfast. They both assured me that neither had left anything on nor had they had their bedroom TVs on in prior nights.

Naturally, when I woke a number of nights later to the same high-speed, high-pitched babble, I got up to seek out the guilty party. But as I wandered the house trying to determine the source, I could find nothing: no television or radio or anything else. Though so faint I sometimes had to strain to hear, the sound or voice or whatever else would describe it followed me from room to room. I would not learn until later what that meant. Apparently,

I was hearing, or was aware of, the extraordinarily high vibration that may accompany spirit activity.

It was around this time that light started to find its way into our night-time hours, first in the form of, for lack of a better description, illuminated cigarette smoke that always seemed to move very quickly and in every direction around the top of the room. Within days of that first unexplained light, fine points of light also began to appear in our bedroom. I refer to these moving points of light as "fireflies." What these different lights had in common is that every time I became aware of them, Tiffany had been very much on my mind. I had seen these things for as long as I can remember but had always attributed them to any very real reason. I chose to not say much about these things, thinking, as many people do, that it perhaps seemed a bit unbelievable.

This changed one evening just after midnight when I lifted my head from my pillow to see the most incredible column of fireflies at the foot of our bed. Sure that nobody could possibly mistake what I was seeing, I woke Lisa. She confessed that while she couldn't see anything she did feel a coldness in the room. She wanted badly to see what I was seeing and I steered her hand into the midst of the small darting lights. Tears came to her eyes as Lisa told me that while she could not see what I did, she felt a coldness and tingling in her hand.

We didn't dare to move, fearing that we would lose what we now both believed was Tiffany coming to visit, so we called to Emma in from her bedroom. She came in and while she could not see anything either, she was able to feel the same things in her hand that Lisa was.

157

Of course, Derek could not be left out so after a number of attempts to call him in, we finally heard him staggering sleepily down the upstairs hallway. We were anxious to know if he would be able to feel the cold and tingling sensations that the girls were but he did us one better. I didn't have time to even say a word to him when he stopped in his tracks at the doorway and almost blurted out, "I see it." I sat a bit confused until I saw what could have been either amazement or fear in his eyes. I asked him what, exactly, it was that he saw.

What he described was the very same thing I was seeing: a small column of tiny pinpoints of light moving quickly about. The four of us sat on the bed, the girls waving a hand in and out and Derek and I simply watching. It was so unreal to us but, at the same time, unmistakable. Understandably, both Derek and Emma were still unnerved well after our lights had faded and spent the remainder of a sleepless night huddled in the same bed.

These experiences have become more intense and also more varied as time has gone on. Since our collective firefly experience, I have seen in Tiffany's room what I can only describe as spinning cocoons of light. These are pure white light, perhaps the size of a bumblebee, that will spin as they move across the room. I could never describe it properly, but to see them, it is as if they are not of this world. That is to say they are sort of in their own element. I can usually expect them now when the candle flame in Tiffany's window starts to dance.

For quite a while after these things began to occur, I still had a difficult time wrapping my head around it. I went so far as to speak to different people who are in the spirit business and they have assured me that what I have experienced is real, though they could not, from their distance, guarantee just who it was that was visiting us.

I don't know about "astralling," whether our subconscious allows us to travel to other places and times while sleeping, as some claim. Nor do I know about spirits drawing their energy from us, but I do think we would be naive to believe that all of life's answers are right there in front of us. I absolutely do not understand everything I have seen but I do know that it gives me hope and maybe that's enough. Maybe that's all there really is to believing in anything.

GRIEVING ...
AND LIFE'S LESSONS

For the longest time, Tiffany wanted our permission to get a tattoo but Lisa and I resisted. When she was seventeen, she added a small tattoo without us knowing. Emma spilled the beans to us the next day. Tiffany died still holding on to her secret.

When I sat down to write this chapter, I did just that – I sat. I sat for a long time before I realized there are no words that can describe the grief after losing a child. I suppose I really knew this all along. The past two years have been incredibly difficult, but I believe now there is also more to losing a child than just grief. I don't think it is possible for someone to walk away from any negative or horrific experience without finding some kind of lesson, or taking some kind of knowledge away.

I know that within our household, we look at life from a much different place now than most people. As a result of Tiffany's death, I have learned to re-evaluate, or perhaps more to the point, re-value the things in my life. I think often of these things now. There are truly things that, three years ago, I put much more value on than I do now. This is the case with a number of different aspects: material things, friends and relationships and family. Certainly, I would never claim to have all of life's answers but I have learned exactly what is most important to us now.

If we all sat down to really think about it, it would come as no surprise for us to realize that we live in a culture that is driven by the need for material things or a desire for superiority. Human vanity and the constant search for power and influence dictate many behaviours. And the result is never beneficial. Let's think about it. There are probably enough resources on the planet right now to sustain everyone on it. But no matter what the cost – profit, power, irreversible pollution, and even death and destruction through war – some people cannot survive without their thirty million per year or owning their own small country.

And it scales down to much more simplistic applications. What make of car or having a bigger home seem to be so important to some. I like my truck but I'm pretty sure that I can't take it with me when I die. Now that I think about it, if someone else owned my truck, I'd probably like it much less.

I recall taking Derek to a spring hockey tournament just a couple of months after Tiffany's death. The elitist mentality hit me flat in the face as soon as we walked through the arena doors. It occurred to me then that there are parents out there who are more concerned that their child be a better goaltender or soccer player or piano player than they are a person.

These are things that have truly been placed in a

greater perspective for me. I mentioned earlier that I tend to watch people even more now than I did before. I watch how people treat each other, both their friends and their families. With regard to friends, I appreciate those relationships much more these days. I don't see these people every day or, in many cases, as often as I would like but I know that they are there. How does the saying go? Your friends are the people who treat you the same whether you are in the room or not.

I am a bit ashamed to say this but I truly believe, even with the pain I still have, that I am a better parent now than I was before Tiffany's passing. I know that loving your children should be the easiest and most natural thing in the world for us as parents but some still manage to screw it up. I read or watch the news now and there are so many – too many – stories about teen swarmings or teens stealing cars or anything else. What all of these young people have in common is that they are all somebody's children. (I also know that those parents are also somebody's children.)

Again, it is my own opinion, but raising our children is one of life's events that we want to get right before the opportunity is gone. We only get one chance. I often hear parents complaining of the "sacrifices" they make for their children and it confuses me. Maybe that's a problem. Sacrifice should be something we want to achieve and not something to regret or be pitied.

These are things I've learned since Tiffany's death. In some cases, they are things I've always known but have been reenforced. There are so many other things I have learned since Tiffany's death. I think her death helped to teach me. We all need to learn from the people in our lives, and Tiffany was one of my best teachers.

It is the grief of Tiffany's death that is front and centre, however. No matter what I write in the pages ahead about the grief we have and still feel, the words will still look cold in print. I don't believe that anyone who hasn't been there will truly understand this grieving process. I can say this because I was once one of those people. I know that after Tiffany's death, I began to read almost anything I could find written by parents who have lost a child, whether it was how their child had died or how they dealt with the time afterward. I know that others sharing their stories has helped me to know that I wasn't going through this alone.

I had never thought a lot about the grieving process other than to say I had been through it a number of times. I didn't know about unconscious emotions or thoughts, that we cannot help the way we feel. I have always had days when I felt sadness, days of total apathy. I had experienced anger or desperation. When I had a conscious mind to do so, I could usually take a pretty good guess at the source of those emotions but really, I simply chose not to analyze them much. Sometimes we just wake up in a good mood or a bad one without ever thinking why.

Tiffany's death changed that thinking. In the past two years, when I have days when I am overwhelmed by sadness or anger or confusion, I don't try to get away from them. I think that they are necessary. Those feelings fall within the grieving process and trying to get away from them is harmful. I can only stress that this is what I have figured out. I am so aware that everyone is different in the way they grieve.

I have learned from Tiffany's death how you grieve does matter. Everyone is truly different in the way they deal with emotions or stages of their grief, and that is the difference. A grieving parent cannot rely on one written or prescribed way to grieve. Some people in mourning may seek the church or their God to help them through. Many will seek professional help and some rely on the friendly ears of friends who are equipped to listen.

I've heard it said that the amount a person grieves for a loved one is directly proportional to the amount they loved. I believe that. I truly believe that Lisa has struggled much more than any of us because of her incredible love for Tiffany. The two of them had a bond, they were attached to each other. Lisa has told me that in the only encounter she has had since Tiffany's death, she felt, and is convinced, that Tiff has hugged her. I know how difficult losing Tiffany has been for me. I know that even now, Lisa has moments when she wishes she could be with Tiffany, wherever that may be. I am wakened too often by her nightmares. And I know she sometimes believes she is no longer a good enough mother to Derek and Emma. That is also so difficult for her. It crushes me to know that Lisa's pain has been so devastating. Her emotional torture is, in its way, more intense than my own.

I also truly believe that the process, those seventeen days, we went through is perhaps more complicated than some. The fact that we were so beaten down by Tiffany's having been missing for such a long time and the days of searching for her only added to our suffering. I had mentioned that when Lisa and I arrived at the canal in February, the day after Tiffany went missing, we knew in our hearts that she was in the canal. As a parent, you try to hold on to any hope you can. As the days went on, however, even the authorities admitted she was in the water somewhere. At that point, the issue became knowing or not knowing if we would ever get to bring her home to say goodbye. These were times of torture for us. When we would eventually get the telephone call telling us of her being found, I suppose there may have been relief in a small way but our family was already emotionally drained, almost as though we had no immune system to try to cope.

In the weeks and months immediately after Tiffany's funeral, time stood still for us. Our sadness and depression were paralyzing. Nothing mattered. Lisa and I craved sleep because it would take the pain away if only for a little while. When not in a restless sleep, we could only sit or lie on the couch and do nothing. It was too difficult to even hold a thought. After a time, other emotions began to creep in. We would have days of bitterness. Lisa couldn't understand how the world could just go on without Tiffany in it. How could people just go on with their own lives when ours was being torn apart?

For my part, I was bitter for different reasons. I was angry, and at no one in particular, for Tiffany's best years being stolen. She was just coming into what would have been the best times of her life. Discovering the woman she would be, falling in love, and all the learning that comes with the early adult years. Tiffany would never see those young years. Let's face it, of all the teens and younger folks I've ever coached, none of them has ever said, "I can't wait to be a senior citizen."

I had also felt actual bitterness towards others who had lost a child, perhaps through a terminal illness or an accident, but who had an opportunity to say goodbye. I recall thinking of how I would have given anything to sit with Tiffany, or to hold her one last time and tell her how much we loved her, how important she was to us, and to thank her for her teachings. I actually envied those parents who had that chance. I cannot speak for my wife, but I felt cheated. I am completely aware of how selfish that sounds and I can only say I do not feel that way now, but in those first weeks, we were both bitter. Perhaps that bitterness really was overflow from the anger we felt at Tiffany being taken from us so early. Perhaps it stemmed from guilt.

Lisa and I asked ourselves for the longest time what we could have done to still have Tiffany with us. Could we have refused to let her go to work in Hamm? Could we have forbidden her to paddle? We even asked ourselves why we weren't in Hamm to help her that day. None of these questions would be fair or reasonable now but again, there wasn't much rational thinking in the time following Tiffany's death.

More than any other emotion, Lisa and I were freefalling into the deepest depression and enduring all of the by-products that come with that state. The sadness was so overwhelming. We were missing Tiffany so very much. We always will. The pain of what we had lost was a constant that only periodic sleep would take away. We had many days of feeling complete helplessness. We had no idea how to proceed with our lives or where or what we should do, not only in the short term, but in the years ahead. I've heard it said we should try to be grateful for the time we had with Tiff and to celebrate that. Perhaps that may happen at some point in the future but for the time being, that is much easier said than done.

Things were made a little more difficult, I think, perhaps by the way that Lisa and I differ in the way we deal with our emotions. We often have the same reactions to circumstance or events but the way we present those reactions is vastly different.

Lisa, in the almost forty years that I have known her, has always been very guarded. She is a true thinker and has traditionally given very little away as to what might be going on inside.

I am different in that regard. I am very much a live-in-the-moment type of person and can be easily distracted at times. I tend to talk about the feelings I am having or, at the very least, wear my heart very much on my sleeve.

This has made it more difficult for Lisa and me to connect. Talking about Tiff's death was further complicated by the fact that we were terrified to bring up anything to each other that might increase each other's pain. As a result, we did not talk to each other enough about Tiffany's death during the immediate time afterward. I was still battling my own demons from Hamm and some of my days there.

It was weeks after Tiffany's death when Lisa would make that awful confession to me that she did not want to be alive. She wasn't going to end her own life and had no thoughts of doing so. She just wanted to be with Tiffany. She knew Derek and Emma would be fine with me so that thought, I suppose, came easier. At first, Lisa was able to find a doctor who was able to help her a little bit, but even that was minimal. Though she was able to talk through her feelings, it still couldn't bring back what she truly needed; she needed Tiffany back. It wouldn't be until months later that Lisa would be able to find a doctor and a support group that would be truly helpful. Mothers of Angels, a group for mothers who have lost children, has given Lisa a safe haven to cope with Tiffany's death.

It would also not be until months later that I even realized I wasn't coping. I was trying so hard to be that husband and father – the everything that my family needed me to be – I didn't make time for my own grief. I don't think now that it was a conscious thing, just reaction. According to close friends, I seemed to be okay with talking about Tiffany's death and the seventeen days following. I wonder now if I was too comfortable.

After the fiasco that spending the weekend away for Tiffany's birthday proved to be, we began to dread other upcoming family gatherings. We could not envision Christmas or other family celebrations without having Tiffany with us. For all that we have been through, our family has been there every step of the way.

The odd time that I've thought about it, I cannot even comprehend how anyone could possibly survive such devastating traumas on their own, without the help and support of anyone close. Lisa and I have been maintained by the loving relationships we have with our family and friends. When in the company of those relationships, we are held up and we can be maintained. Unfortunately, those relationships are not available to us at night and without them, the grief is all that we see.

I have always known we are all different in the way we cope with the things life hands us. It would be the same in trying to determine which coping mechanisms work best for us. Lisa and I have sought out various types of help, and it may take a while to find these things. We also received a bit of help in November of '06 when Scottie, our now one-hundred-and-ten-pound Bernese Mountain "puppy," came to us. He has been such a wonderful distraction for us and has given Lisa something to love when she desperately needed it. These sources have been a saviour of sorts for Lisa. They have enabled her to at least peek up over the edge of the bottomless hole she is in.

We both believe we should be farther along than we are or "getting better," and perhaps people outside might expect it. We know that a parent can never be whole again after they have lost a child. There is no timetable for grief, and everyone travels their own path and at their own speed.

As for me, I am fortunate that I was able to find friends who had it within themselves to simply sit and listen to me talk about Tiffany. From her growing years, to the day she was found in the Datteln-Hamm canal to where I am now, they have been kind and loyal enough to allow me to use them. There were times, I think, when I perhaps wanted or needed others to feel our pain or to know how much Lisa and I were hurting. Really, this is not possible and not at all fair.

I have tried to be aware of the kindness of these friends and not to overtax it. It would be the worst possible thing for me if I were to make people so tired of hearing of Tiffany that they would begin to resent her and to want to run when they saw me coming. Ultimately, I really believe that it is vitally important to seek out whatever sources of help you can find, regardless of how guarded you have always been. There are people out there who are able to help, even if it is only to listen. Search those people out.

A very good friend actually sought me out not long after Tiffany's death and she posed the following question: "If you could have anything or have knowledge of any one thing, what would it be?"

I didn't even have to think about an answer. I would want what every grieving parent would want short of having their child back. If I could know, and know for absolute certain, that Tiffany was in a safe place, that she was okay, and that she was truly happy, things might be easier for us. My friend then wrote the most amazing letter to Lisa and me, essentially stating that through her own contact with God, she knew that Tiffany was in a good place.

WHERE WE ARE NOW

Perhaps as a symptom of being so shy, Tiff's hand-writing was so small, we sometimes needed a mag-nifying glass to read it. Seriously.

So where am I now? Where are we as a family? I can write about all of the things that we feel now as a family. I can write about our sadness, our helplessness, and about the most intense pain of grief, even two years later. But really, once you as a reader have left these words on the page, you will have forgotten them in an hour's time. Our pain will go on and on. We so often hear, after the death of a loved one, that "time heals" or that "things will get better with time." And I do believe that. But I am also very sure that the one exception to that rule is losing a child. It is only my opinion and based on my own experiences, but our pain has refused to subside as time has gone by.

In many ways, we are actually in a much more difficult place now than we were in the immediate time following Tiffany's funeral. Understandably, we were still in a fog, a state of disbelief, for months. Tiffany's death still wasn't real. In those first days, I can even remember that on some, I would think to myself, I can't wait until things get back to normal, things will be better when Tiffy comes home, as if she really would.

But as that fog lifted it has revealed the realization that this truly is final: Tiffany's death, that time cannot be altered or changed, and she is not coming home. Add to this reality the fact that as time goes on, Tiff gets farther away from us. Memories start to lose their vividness.

The time since Tiffany's death has taken its toll on our family. Really, the biggest differences in our family are the ones nobody sees. Tiffany is all we think about before we are able to sleep at night and the first thought we have when we wake in the morning.

I do all that I can to try to keep her as close to me as possible. I still walk the path she and I used to take when we would walk home from her elementary school together. I still drive to the stable where Tiff took riding lessons, just to "pick her up" and then I drive home again. And I talk with her now as we did then.

A customer of mine commented to me not long ago that I "seemed to be dealing with it." Perhaps on the outside. Even on days when I'm able to work and I think of Tiffy, it is still hard to catch my next breath. Although I do this less frequently now, there were many nights when I would go into their rooms in the early morning hours and just sit with Derek and Emma, just to be near them. On many nights, Emma had cried herself to sleep. They are still carrying their respective rocks. Both have started new schools now, and with that comes new distractions so they are able to put that weight aside a bit more.

In October of 2008, I returned to Hamm on my own. I felt I needed to do this for two reasons in particular. My dreams, or nightmares, of that March evening when I was sure I had found Tiffany had been coming both much more frequently and much more vividly.

The actual time that I had my hand on what I believed was Tiffany was very short. Every emotion that was with me that night was being brought back. That night brought the most incredible levels of fear, panic, confusion, dread, and so much more. Those moments had taken me to a cold and awful place, both literally and figuratively.

My mind was not my own that night and I truly believed if I could revisit that one spot, if I could see it in the light of day, it may not seem so bad. Perhaps my recollections and impressions might somehow be altered or changed into something I could better cope with.

For October, the day I returned was remarkably warm and clear. Folks were walking throughout the city in shirt sleeves. The area was not terribly difficult to locate. I was quiet now, nothing screaming through my head.

I was able to sit on the canal bank, with the sun on my face, listening to the flow of the water. It was so calm. There was no more feeling of dread or panic. Now it was only sadness of what we have lost and not so much how we lost. But under any other circumstance, the area was not an awful place to be now. It was calm and peaceful and I made it a point that day to bring that memory home with me.

The second reason for my return to Hamm may sound just a bit odd to some. As time had gone by, I felt Tiff moving farther and farther away from me. As strange as it sounds, the last place I had felt connected to Tiffany

was walking the banks of the canal, when it was just Tiff
and me and nobody else. My entire focus was on Tiffany. I walked the banks again in October and was able to
be with Tiff. Again, there was no panic or fear this time.
There was only sadness but my memories of her were not
difficult to find.

I still sit in Tiffany's room late into the night. I am
very aware that death has a "smell" for me now. Very often, when I am in Tiff's room, I am aware of that same
smell I remember from the undertaker's in Hamm. It is
not an unpleasant thing but it is very specific for me –
and something that didn't exist in Tiff's room before she
left us.

The last thing I do every night before going to bed is
light a candle in her bedroom window, touch my fingers
to her picture that sits on a shelf there, and then I wish
her goodnight and I remind her of how much we love
and miss her. This is something I know I will do for the
rest of my life.

In the meanwhile, neither Lisa nor I have any energy
or motivation; there are days when just sitting is all that
we can do. Those days are often accompanied by confusion and still, sometimes, anger … always, in the plainest,
simplest words, an awareness that life just sucks. We want
life to be better and be able to smile a little more often,
but we just don't know how to get there. Perhaps some-
day. Lisa verbalizes a little more now than in the earlier
days but it is still just intense pain for her. I still see the
pain on her face even while she sleeps. We are learning to
cope; we have to. But we will never again have a normal
existence. That is not possible for anyone who has ever
lost a child. And for all those parents who have, my honest and deepest sympathies.

Thank You

There are many people our family is grateful to for their support, compassion, and prayer both during our ordeal and in the months since. They include:

All of the rescue workers, divers, police officers, firefighters, water police and anyone involved in the search for our daughter during those first seventeen days.

Tiffany's German family for all they have done for our family and for sharing our pain.

Angus Borland for his friendship and support in Germany.

Hamm police officer Marcus Tiemann for his compassion and support then and now.

Christine Hoehne for her help with communication and translation.

Brad Murray of Air Canada for arranging flights to and from Germany at only a moment's notice.

The Air Canada Concierge staff in Frankfurt, London, Montreal, Toronto, and Halifax for the kindness, respect and compassion shown to us during our travel back and forth.

Air Canada concierge Carol Baldwin both for her diligence in helping with travel and Customs arrangements as well as her time to "rescue me."

Rita Meuller and the club officials and membership of the Datteln-Hamm kayak club for their generosity and compassion.

Lisa's mom and sisters for their unending love and support.

David MacDonald, Donna and Don Shewfelt for their friendship and setting up trust accounts for Tiffany.

Tina, Jerry, Ashley, and the late Mary-Beth Chaulk, Steve and Wendy Rethy, Paula and Bill Yochoff, Steven Tanner of Metro Transit for their fund-raising efforts.

Morneau Sobeco for its kind and generous donation.

Citizens of the City of Hamm.

Pete for lending me her ears and time.

And all those (too many to mention) who made donations to the Scotia Bank account.

Most of all, we are grateful to the community in which we live for the most incredible support during our time of grief. The constant support, prayer and compassion will always be remembered and appreciated.

* * *

In the months after Tiffany's death, our then eleven-year-old daughter Emma worked to set up a website both to honour Tiff as well as to enable any who desired a forum to leave messages for Tiffany and/or her family. The site address is www.tiffanyrip.piczo.com. Emma has also set up a Facebook group called RIP Tiffany Tanner.

* * *

Our family has established a scholarship fund in Tiffany's name. The scholarship is awarded annually to a graduating student from Prince Andrew High School or Dartmouth High School. If anyone would like to make a donation, cheques may be made payable to the Halifax Regional School Board with the Tiffany Tanner Scholarship Fund noted on the cheque, and can be sent to me at 82 Lorne Avenue, Dartmouth, Nova Scotia, B2Y 3E7. We will ensure it is deposited to Tiffany's fund and a tax receipt will be issued to the donor.